GLIMPSES

OF

REAL LIFE.

BY THE

AUTHOR OF "THE BURNISH FAMILY."

GLASGOW:
SCOTTISH TEMPERANCE LEAGUE.
LONDON: HOULSTON & WRIGHT; W. TWEEDIE.
EDINBURGH: WM. OLIPHANT & CO.; J. MENZIES;
OLIVER & BOYD.
MANCHESTER: WILLIAM BREMNER.

PRICE SIXPENCE.

GLIMPSES

OF

REAL LIFE.

BY THE

AUTHOR OF "THE BURNISH FAMILY."

———————————

GLASGOW:

SCOTTISH TEMPERANCE LEAGUE.

LONDON: HOULSTON & WRIGHT, AND W. TWEEDIE.

MACKAY AND KIRKWOOD, PRINTERS, GLASGOW.

CONTENTS.

THE THREE MEETINGS.

On a moonlight night, in June 184—, a young man, to whom we might safely give the often misapplied term of gentleman, issued with a hasty step from the gate of a public garden in the western suburbs of the metropolis. He walked quickly along a lane that led into the open road, and towards an old bridge on the right that spanned the Thames, the highway to some marshy fields, which might well be called the Lowlands of Surrey. The student of human character knows there is a great deal of individuality in the tread, as well as the walk of people. Our pedestrian's foot struck the ground impatiently, and the half disdainful swing of his shoulders and erect bearing of his head, quite as much as his kindling cheek and eyes, indicated strong if not deep emotion. As soon, however, as he reached the old bridge, his pace slackened. He leaned against the rails, and, removing his hat, pushed his thick, dark hair from his forehead, as if to cool or calm his brain with the soft, night air. It would not have been easy for the most perturbed spirit to resist the soothing influence of such a night. The moon had filled the unclouded heavens with her light, and the river at high tide, now really " the silver Thames," with its soft ripple, looked the very emblem of tranquillity. Even the houses on the banks seemed to sleep, and the old square tower of a neighbouring church—ugly enough by day-light—stood out in bold relief against the clear sky, a massive and venerable object. While the young man glanced from the deep shadows of the old wooden piers of the bridge up to the ancient tower, its clock struck eleven. Suddenly the quiet of the night was further broken by a loud explosion, and a multi-

A

tude of fireworks rose from among the trees on a verdant
little cape that stretched into the river. The shouts and
cheers of voices softened by distance, mingled with the
concussion, and seemed to jar upon the listener's ear, for he
exclaimed as he put on his hat, " It was a fool's pleasure
foolishly taken. There's drunken infamy enough in the
streets of this great Babel, without giving time and money
to make one of a sensual rabble in *that* place." The self-
reproach of the young man, as he resumed his walk, was
suddenly interrupted by sounds of distress. It was not a
scream or shout, but a low subdued voice near, that, in the
extreme of agony was sobbing, " Oh, father, father, dear
father, don't—pray, pray, don't !" There seemed a struggle
going on, and the words, in a husky tone, " Keep off, I tell
you "—" Let me go "—" I'll bear it no longer "—broke in
upon the convulsive sobs of the first speaker. A few strides
brought the young man to the centre of the bridge, in the
recess of which he saw the slight form of a girl clinging
round a man who seemed endeavouring to throw himself
over. A glance sufficed to comprehend the scene; and in
far less time than it has taken us to describe it, the young
man's vigorous hand was on the shoulder of the frantic
wretch, and his voice was exclaiming, " Man ! what do you
mean by this madness ?"   " Oh, Sir, save him—pray hold
him, but don't hurt him, Sir! he's very, very ill. Dear
father, you're better now ? " gasped the young girl. As she
uttered these disjointed sentences she had taken one of the
maniac's arms, and held it fast locked in both hers, while
her bonnet, loosened in the struggle, fell back, and revealed
a face, pale, indeed, with horror, and thin to attenuation,
yet, with the unmistakable stamp of youth and high intelligence upon it. Her abundant, light hair gleamed in the
moonlight, as she fell upon her father's bosom, and tears
choked her utterance. Meanwhile the man writhed in the
grasp of our pedestrian, and glared at him with eyes that
seemed to emit sparks of fire, while his worn features and
wasted limbs quivered convulsively. He tried to speak, but
could not; presently, as he seemed falling to the ground, the
young man looked about for help, and the word " police "
was escaping his lips, when the girl, suddenly looking up,

piteously said, "Oh, don't call the police—don't expose my poor father's misery." "Why, what can I do better for you both? You cannot manage him." "Sir," replied the girl, making a strong effort at composure, "my father has long been ill of a painful disease, and to-night—something troubled him—and—and—he was—that is, pain threw him into a frenzy. He's quiet now, though very weak; will you, Sir, kindly help me to lead him home, we live quite near?"

The young man looked earnestly at the girl as she spoke, and evidently his compassion was struggling with his caution. A stranger in London, he feared imposture everywhere, in the streets most of all; and, as if to strengthen that fear, a group of half-tipsy revellers from the gardens, came singing and shouting on the bridge, and, pausing to look at the sick man now nearly helpless between his daughter and the stranger, they all burst into a wild laugh, "Oh, the sick dodge," said one; "Drunk enough," cried another; "The girl's hardly well up in the part," scoffed a third; and on they went, their worthless words impressing the young man with the belief that he was aiding two well-known vagabonds. However, assistance from the police was not to be had, just then, for the disorderly multitude dismissing from the gardens claimed all the help, or control, the police could give, the persons and property of decent people being left meanwhile to shift for themselves. With a strong hand, but an averted and half-angry glance, the young man crossed the bridge with his strange companions, the feeble form of the girl's father becoming every moment more helpless, and requiring all the strength that both conductors could employ to keep him up between them. At the toll-gate the cheery voice of its stalwart keeper hailed the girl with—"Oh, so you *did* find him. Well! I was bothered with some drunken chaps in a cab, and I s'pose he must have got through then, for I never clapt eyes on him, to my knowledge." While he spoke he put some coppers in the girl's hand, adding, "There's your change, you was off just now like a bird, afore I could give it you." A few paces along the road brought our group to a dismal lane on the right, where a row of hovels led towards a huge factory, whose pungent odour proclaimed it to be chemical works.

Into the broken gateway of the dusty patch of ground, where a few weeds struggled for life, the party entered; but as the girl opened the door, which indeed seemed to have been unfastened, the stranger paused on the threshold, and lifting the man over the broken step put him into the passage. "Hold him, Sir, one moment, please, while I get a light." "No, my good girl, you are at home now, I must go." As he took his arms from the man, before the girl could break the fall, the invalid, with a heavy groan, was prostrate in the passage. The distress of the daughter, and the helplessness of the father, were so real that it was impossible to avoid helping them further. In a few moments, the girl brought a light, and the insensible man was carried or dragged by them into a little room on the right, where, amid a strange confusion of broken furniture and crockery-ware, stood a truckle bed, across the foot of which lay a woman in torn and dabbled garments, sleeping the deep, snoring, brutal sleep of intemperance. If the youth had wished to get away before, this sight increased his desire to be well rid of his strange companions. So, placing the man in an old easy chair, he turned towards the door, saying, "I will call your neighbours to you."

"Thank you for your help, Sir," said the girl, "but call no one—I can manage my father here—he often faints, and we want no spectators of our misery."

There was something in the manner and tone in which this was said, so hopelessly sad, that, spite of himself, the young man lingered while the girl, as if mechanically, applied some restorative to the lips and temples of the sufferer.

"Have you any medical advice for your father? He is very ill, and the scene of to-night proves that he needs more care and help than you can give him. He would be better in an hospital than here."

As he spoke the young man's eye glanced with disdain at the human heap on the bed, and the young girl, with a deep blush, that strangely contrasted with her recent paleness, hastily threw an old shawl over the sleeper, and hid the bloated face from view, as she replied, "He would, I know, be better anywhere—anywhere than here; but I know no subscriber to an hospital, and a letter is necessary."

"I'll give you a name," said the young man, and taking out his pencil, he asked for paper, but the confusion of the place, and the cares of the young girl for the sufferer, added to some muttered indications that the sleeper on the bed was rousing, determined him not to wait, so he wrote, on a card that he drew from his pocket, the name of a subscriber to the Westminster Hospital, and without waiting for further question, or thanks, departed.

As he stepped out of the fetid room, reeking with inde-scribable odours, into the pure, calm moonlight, he seemed emerging into another world. "Oh, holy God!" he ex-claimed, "maker of this beautiful world, and thou hast made these creatures also for thy glory!" As he mused, a decent poor woman interrupted him: "S'cuse me, Sir, didn't you help home poor Mr. Mallery just now?"

"I helped home a sick man, who seemed in the frenzy of a fever to have run over the bridge."

"Ah, Sir! That man's what I calls a martyr, and the wust of martyrs. Hee's wife's a killing of him, bit by bit, and the poor young body, too."

"How so, what is he?"

"Hee's a hoperative chemist, Sir, earns fust rate wages when hee's well, an as done for yeers. My hold man's worked hunder him, and valys him above a bit. An as for Annie Mallery, you may look at a mile of young gals, and won't find one to come up to her. But the wife, Sir, drinks! Ah, she jist does drink! Why, she'd drink the Thames dry, if it was but gin. This very night she was brought home by a police-man, all the boys in the place a hooting of her; and as soon as she got in, she broke every thing she could lay hands on, and abused the sick man in his bed—the brute that she is! till they say he got up and crawled out, though he hasn't put foot to ground afore for a month; and when poor Annie —Miss Annie! I ought to call her—come in from her teaching poor thing! for you see, Sir, by her teaching she keeps them —she found the place all torn to bits, her father gone, and that ere cretur, her mother, or least ways her mother-in-lawr, sprawling mad on the bed."

"My good woman, you will do well to go to the help of the young girl, she has more on her hands this night than she

can manage—say *I* sent you,—*I*, the person that helped her
father home; and, here," putting a coin into the woman's
hand, "there's something for your trouble."

"My trouble! I want nothing. I'd often help 'em if
they'd let me. Howsomever I'll spend the money for 'em;
and many thanks, Sir. You're but young, Sir—'scuse me,
but I've a fine lad of my hone far away, Sir; and I can't
help saying, for his sake like, out of a mother's heart as it
were—Fight shy of the drink, Sir. It's the wust temptation
of all, both to gentle and simple. It begins all gay and
pleasant, like them gardens over the bridge, and it ends in a
leap in the river, or a rotten den like these here, or wus—
fight shy of it."

There was an honesty of purpose in the homely words;
and, though the young man's mind, at the name of "mother!"
was filled, in strong contrast to the speaker, with the image of
a lovely being, now an angel in heaven; for her sweet sake he
gave the rough hand a hearty shake, and with a quivering lip
and moistened eye turned and went his way, and without further interruption reached his lodgings.

Honour to the true word, however roughly spoken!
There's life in it, just as there's life in the husky, unsightly
seed. The listener's heart that night opened to the admonition, and treasured it up; it took root, and became a strong
principle. "She's right," he said, as he retired to rest, "the
use of strong drink is weakness in the beginning, wickedness
and ruin in the end. I will 'fight shy' of it."

While he was sleeping the refreshing sleep of health and
peace, Annie Mallery, yet watching her father, examined the
card the stranger had given her, and saw not only the subscriber's name, but that of Mr. Frederick Linton, engraved
on it—which latter, she rightly judged, was the name of her
unknown friend. It seemed familar to her, but after racking
her memory in vain, she could not recall where or when she
had heard it before.

❖   ❖   ❖   ❖   ❖   ❖   ❖

The events of that night had passed like a painful dream
from the young man's memory, when they were recalled
shortly after by his encountering the young girl, or, properly

speaking, Annie Mallery, in the hall of Westminster hospital. "Oh, they have followed my advice," said he, mentally, "and brought the man here." Annie blushed deeply as she passed him, and for a moment hesitated, as if she wished, yet feared to speak to him. Her timidity conquered, she bent to him respectfully, and with a lingering step mounted the stairs that led to the sick wards on the men's side of the building. After a moment's hesitation, the young man (who was a medical student, in his first session), keeping her in view, followed slowly, and saw that she went up to a bed now surrounded by a screen at the end of a long ward, which was chiefly occupied by physician's patients,—a circumstance that accounted for his not having seen the man, as his studies at present were among the surgical cases. Nor, indeed, would he have recognized the sufferer—it was the young girl's countenance that had impressed his memory, as something rare and spiritual, yet painful.

As he now, following her footsteps, stood at the bedside of the sick man, and exactly opposite to Annie, it needed not the practised eye of a medical man to detect that the shadows of death were gathering over the glazing eye, and the world was fast receding from the relaxed hand that, feeble as an infant's, fell rather than lay on the bed quilt. His daughter, startled by the signs of approaching dissolution, bent over him tenderly, yet alarmed, put down her young face to his caressingly. He did not see her. "Father," she said, "'tis I, Annie—your own poor Annie—pray, speak to me!"

There is no knowing into what mysterious depths of his being that voice penetrated, but it seemed as if his departing soul was arrested for a moment on the threshold of eternity, and struggled with the grasp of death. The rigid features relaxed, big drops stood upon the clammy forehead, and a hollow but perfectly distinct voice said—"My dear child! I am glad you're come; it's very dark. I can't see you, Annie, but I want you to forgive your poor father; I couldn't go, my pet! till I heard you say you'd forgive me for ever putting that—that woman—poor soul, over you."

"Oh, I've nothing to forgive, don't speak, or you'll break my heart; you've been the kindest and best of fathers to me; 'tis I that want forgiveness; for, in all your griefs, you've grieved most for me, dear father! let us both ask God's forgiveness."

The dying man, with a great effort, rose on his elbow, and exclaimed, " I have, child! and He does not forsake me, and He will bless——" there was a grey tint like a cloud passed over the face, the head fell heavily on his kneeling daughter's bosom, and with a short, quick gasp the spirit fled.

The death of this man had been expected and prepared for, in the usual routine of the attendant nurse's day's work, indeed Annie was there at an hour when visitors were not usually admitted, because it was known her father was dying. Not by any means unkindly, but in a very matter-of-course way, the poor girl was led into an adjoining room, and left to compose herself. Frederick Linton longed to follow her, and to utter the expressions of sympathy that he felt; but respect for her friendlessness and her grief kept him back. He wished, as a pure-minded young man would do, that he had a sister or some female relative whom he could interest in the orphan, for he knew, and the chivalry of his nature respected the restriction that he could not, without subjecting the poor girl to invidious remarks, manifest any deep concern about her. Besides, he was not rich. He had been, for some years, studying his profession with his father, a surgeon in Yorkshire, a man who, after the death of Frederick's mother, consoled himself by living fully up to his income; and, though long in practice, could but just afford to complete the medical education of his son by sending him to study in London for a few years. He meant, ultimately, to have him as a partner in his practice. Meanwhile he kept him on rather short allowance, for a spendthrift is seldom generous to his own family.

A week after the death-bed scene, our student yielding to a better impulse than mere curiosity, walked to the dwelling where he had witnessed such misery, and was surprised to find it deserted. On inquiry of the fruit woman who sat at a stall at the corner, he recognized by her voice his monitor of the former night. " Ah, death's door was long a-opening —it always is for them as wants to go, but it's let him out of his misery at last. But the poor young body's no better off. That ere woman 'll stick to her. Just now she's been an promised to reform, and Miss Annie believed her. So, to take her away from this place, where her drinking was know'd, the daughter has took a lodging somewhere tother side of the bridge—but she'll be as bad there." "Why, do you say that? she may mend." "Not she. If she gave up the drink entirely she might, but she'll never mend upon her little drops—no more than a smoky chimley 'll mend by my puffing the fire. That woman has got Miss Annie out of two good schools where she taught; by going there drunk and disgracing the poor thing, and she'll get her out of the family where she's a daily gov'ness now, if she does but find where they lives, but Miss Annie walks a round-about way, morning and night, so that she mayn't be watched; but drunkards bean't all stoopid, some's cunning, and that's her kind."

Frederick Linton did not stay to hear the definition of the different kinds of drunkards. He ascertained that no information was to be gained as to the present abode of the young person who had interested him, and, moreover, that she was not in actual want, and thanking his humble but sensible acquaintance, and heaving a sigh at the troubles that probably lay before the young teacher, he departed.

❁   ❁   ❁   ❁   ❁   ❁   ❁

Four years had passed since the incidents recorded took place, and Frederick Linton had become not only his father's assistant, but that father's recent death had made him his successor. His practice lay among the scattered villages that surrounded a remote Yorkshire town. Long rides by day and night over wild moors and through lonely valleys were common to him. But his health, preserved by genuine temperance, (which does not mean tampering with an evil, but abolishing it,) bore him well through his fatigues; and his promptitude, sympathy, and cheerfulness, as well as professional ability, made him a general favourite; more particularly, it must be owned, in families where there were daughters to marry. A distant cousin of Frederick's made up, on the death of his father, for long neglect by profuse civilities, and as her house lay very much in the way of his most frequent rides, he often dropped in, to the great delight of the lady, who was one of the most famous match-makers of the district. Not that she had daughters to marry, but she liked to impress her young friends with the idea that Frederick asked her advice and deferred to her judgment, than which nothing could be more false ; for though a young man of twenty-five could not be expected to equal a subtile woman ten years his senior in the art of manœuvring, yet, he had the honest instinct which shrinks involuntarily from all that is not fair and open.

Mrs. Gloss was fond of consulting him on other than professional matters, and one day when he called she began a long complaint about her children's governess, who, she said, "was so reserved and proud, there was no living with her."

Now, Mr. Linton had often heard this governess named by families in the district, and always with commendation. He had never to his knowledge seen her, but he recollected that some beautiful drawings, which were the ornament of a charity bazaar recently held, had been executed by her ; and he wished to know the fair artist. Indeed, once he thought she had shunned him, by retreating swiftly from the garden on the occasion of one of his calls on Mrs. Gloss.

However, he was doomed to hear anything but favourable accounts of her this morning. Mrs. Gloss was very voluble, and talked herself angry. "She's a character ! and I dislike characters, they're so determined to differ from everybody else. Only think, at my own table, of the rudeness of this Miss Nobody, who comes from no-where, that I can learn (for a school recommended her to me), refusing to take wine with our vicar ! who honoured her with his notice, because of those drawings there's such a fuss about. And then, if I gave her time to make drawings for *my* stall at a bazaar, that *I* patronize, I don't choose she shall be sitting up, and getting up, early and late, making drawings, that she packs off without showing me, or consulting me, or anything. And then she's so unlady-like ; only last week she walks off to Huddersfield, certainly I grant it was after she'd done with the children, and goes to the post, and gets letters there, and what's more, sends off money orders from there, and when it comes to my ears, and I go to demand an explanation, I find her crying her eyes out, just as if she was ill-used. I'll have no clandestine doings in my house. I said to her, "If you've low or mysterious connections you wont do to educate my children." "But," at length interposed Mr. Linton, "what reason have you for supposing there is anything wrong in what you allege? a lady who has perhaps suffered a reverse of fortune, may justly have reserves, that only sympathy would induce her to unfold."

"Oh, stuff, Fred, you're romantic; what sympathy can she want more than I give her? I'm always inquiring of her about her friends, and not a word can I get from her. She teaches the children well, and they improve, or I would not keep her a day."

Just then a little girl ran into the room with a bit of paper in her hand.

"Oh, ma, look at this, there was an old man talking to our governess last night over the hedge at the bottom of the garden; and just now while we were there at play we picked up this, and we don't know whether it's for you or her."

"An old man! What old man?" said the mother, clutching the paper. "From the workhouse, mamma; he had the union coat on."

The scrawl ran thus:—"Daughter, I'm ill with toiling to find you out, and I'm put into the workhouse here; I desire, if you've a spark of gratitude or feeling, that you come to me. I saw you in all your grandeur at church on Sunday, and I know the people you're with; so unless you want an exposure, come to me at once, for I can't and won't live the life I do, and you in plenty. Your poor," a rent in the paper cut short the termination of this epistle. Mrs. Gloss's countenance was in a flame as she tossed the letter to Frederick, with the words—"Read that; you did not seem to believe me, cousin, just now."

"Excuse me," was the reply, "I cannot read this unless I know whether it is yours, and that you have had a right to read it."

"Why, it was open, with no address, and it's to this fine piece of hypocrisy that I've been harbouring."

"Then, instantly, cousin, send the young lady her letter; and as you have been so unfortunate as to read it by mistake, apologize for it, and of course you will be silent as to its contents."

"Apologize—silent!—why the creature has a father or mother—a tramp, and now in the workhouse; but I'll go to her instantly, and know the meaning of it."

Mr. Linton's horse was waiting for him, and with a displeased look he left the house, and as he was the parish doctor, rode forward to the workhouse—not certainly without thinking of the strange account he had heard—but with no idea of seeing the man or woman to whom Mrs. Gloss had referred. However, on his arrival, he was called on to visit a new comer who had been found drunk the day before in the road, and in that state had been brought into the house. She had rallied, talked largely of being a reduced lady, and having a daughter very well off in the neighbourhood; and it was known she had bribed one of the paupers to take a note for her to Mrs. Gloss's. During the present day a slight bruise on her face had become very inflamed, and she seemed to be exceedingly ill. The surgeon hastened to the bedside of the miserable woman, who was alternately moaning with pain and asking for drink. "None of your slops, I tell you I can't live without something comforting. You're murdering me if you refuse it. I'll see the doctor." "Well, my good woman, you do see him," said Mr. Linton, stepping to her bedside, "What can I do for you?"

"Order me some brandy, and I shall give you no more trouble, Sir!" was the answer from a woman, bloated, feeble, and prematurely old, on whose face excess had set its deforming stamp, until every feature looked animal. There was the swollen nose, the dropped under lip, cracked with fever, the puffed cheeks, and a bandage over the inflamed forehead. Surely, thought the surgeon, as he looked at this mass, "the way of transgressors is hard."

Yet, as the creature asked and began to rave for strong drink, there was the accent of one who had not always herded with the vile.

The surgeon prescribed for her, for he knew how dangerous were the slightest ailments to persons of such habits as those of the present patient. He left a nurse bathing her head, and went his rounds among the other patients. There were many sick, and his stay was prolonged more than an hour, when before leaving he looked in again on "the tramp," as she was called. At the bed-side, he saw an elegant young woman, very plainly dressed, who was weeping bitterly, while the wretched invalid was reviling her.

"What have you to cry for? You've had the sweets of life, and left me to the sours. You wouldn't live at home with me and be a morning governess: No, no! You must give me the slip, which I must say was mean and unfeeling; and then to expect I could live on the pittance you thought proper to send me in post-office orders! But I've found you, and I'll keep to you, I can tell you. I never deserted you, nor your father; No, I had a better heart, and knew my duty. Oh! I shall go mad with pain. Take me away, I tell you, from this place, or they'll murder me with their slops."

The young woman tried to interpose some soothing words amid the volley of abuse of her tormentor; but when told her life had been "sweet," she raised her eyes to heaven, with such an expression of anguish, as once seen could not be forgotten. At that moment, Frederick Linton saw the uplifted face, and knew it at once. The scene on the bridge, and in the hospital, flashed upon his recollection. "I think we have met before," said he, respectfully approaching her.

"Yes! Mr. Linton, and always in sorrow, but never in greater grief than now—that this poor creature, my father's wife, by her imprudence has caused Mrs. Gloss so to treat me,—that is, to request me to leave her house. Oh! Sir, life is very bitter to me!"

"Linton! who spoke of the Lintons?" said the woman. Her words were unheeded by the weeping girl, and her deeply interested companion. But she reiterated the words,—"Whom did you call Linton?"

"It is my name," said the surgeon, "Why?"

"It was mine. I was Harriet Linton before I married my first husband, Captain Johnson."

"Harriet Linton! What! of Suffolk, the sister of Janet,—Harriet who married and went to America with Captain Johnson, and whom we long thought dead!"

"Yes, I tell you," glared the woman, "I'm that person;—now, for mercy's sake, let me have some brandy! I tell you I must have it."

With a trembling hand the surgeon administered a restorative, which, however, the patient with a grimace put aside.
It's strong, but it's not brandy, and nothing else will do me
any good—nothing else," she said.

"One moment! tell me did you then return from America
a widow, and marry again?"

"Did I! yes; and I never deserted my husband, though
he was poor enough, always taking from me to educate his
girl; and she, yes! I will tell it, ungratefully left me, and
always grudged my little comforts; but I've found her now,
and if I could but find my sister Janet, I should be easy."

"Come this way, Miss Mallery," said Frederick, drawing
the still weeping girl to a window, while the sick woman
raved for drink. A word with you. "Is it correct that this
woman was Harriet Linton?"

"Yes, Sir, but I only remember her as Mrs. Johnson—the
name of Linton struck me as familiar, and I now recollect that
I saw it written in an old pocket Bible that belonged to her."

"Why this, then, is the long-lost sister of Mrs. Gloss—
whose maiden name was Linton. We knew nothing of her
return from America."

Annie knew, though she did not say so much, that the
habits of the woman who for six years embittered her father's
life, and broke his heart, and for ten years had been a curse
to herself, were so irregular that it was no wonder she had
not written. She, however, heard the communication without much interest, for Mrs. Gloss had so smote upon her heart,
by the cruel dismissal she had just given her, that nothing
but time could heal the bruise.

However, Mr. Linton departed instantly, not, to say truth,
unwilling to shame his cousin, who, if she did not feel for
her sister's disgrace would feel for her own. He arrived as
that amiable lady was just telling to two like-minded gossips
—for every circle has its vulgarians—what an impostor she
had harboured—"the daughter of a drunken tramp! to pre-
sume to apply for my situation."

"Pardon me," said Frederick Linton, whose quick ear as
he entered the room, caught the word, "Miss Mallery is not
the daughter of the person in question, she is only related by
marriage."

"But to be related at all—to have such low connections."

"Hush! cousin Janet, hush—you know not that you are reflecting on yourself and me."

"Mr. Frederick Linton," said the lady haughtily, "no one knows better than you, that our family, in all its branches, is respectable. As for me, I have no near relatives. My poor sister who married, imprudently, that delightful Captain Johnson, was the belle of the county—our native Suffolk—and might have had any one. Dear creature! I wish we could get any tidings of her."

"Your wish is granted, she is found."

"Found! What! Where? Fred, tell me what you mean?"

"Just what I say, come with me and I'll show you—the belle of the county."

"Explain yourself, for heaven's sake? Why do you look so strange?"

"The shortest explanation I can give is, that the young lady you have so unceremoniously dismissed is now sitting by a bed, that contains her mother-in-law and your sister; who, it seems, after her widowhood, returned, eleven years back, and married a widower with one daughter, whose name was Mallery."

It is needless to describe the very florid hysterics that followed this announcement, or the mortification of the interview in the workhouse that succeeded. Mrs. Gloss was vain and weak, but perhaps not utterly heartless, and the lesson was salutary, since she never again talked about the sin of having low connections. The miserable woman was removed to Mrs. Gloss's house, and might have recovered, but that her entreaties for brandy were yielded to. Erysipelas set in with great violence, and in three days from the time of her removal, she died raving mad.

Need we tell the sequel? Happiness is soon chronicled. Frederick Linton took the best means to confirm the dismissal which Mrs. Gloss, to her ultimate chagrin had given Annie, for he offered her a home of her own, shackled with the condition, that she should change her name; and such is woman's trust even after the most sorrowful experience, she accepted the offer; both, however, resolving to keep their dwelling unpolluted by strong drink. Mrs. Gloss, who wanted to smooth over certain disagreeables, was loud, if not hearty, in her approval ; and, when she found Annie admired for her intelligence, and loved for her virtues, used always tospeak proudly of her as " her gifted relative."

POLITICS AND PROGRESS AT STOKE-TATLINGTON.

A CERTAIN antique town of the west of England, which we shall call Stoke-Tatlington, used to pride itself, in the old coaching times, on its quietness and gentility. For thirty years it boasted a vicar who was the best whist-player in the county, and whose judgment in wines, horses, and dogs, was pronounced perfect. This good gentleman never puzzled his parishioners with deep, nor wearied them with long sermons; nor did he harass them with frequent services. A perfect repose had settled down upon the grand old church —through whose ivy-mantled windows the morning sunlight softly filtered, and as the broken rays struggled tremulously through and touched the dim emblazonings of the old tombs, or streamed along the stately aisles, deepening by contrast the sombre shadows beneath the arches, the light and shade blended into a kind of dreamy twilight—certainly far more appropriate to a mausoleum for the dead than a meeting place of the living. However, it was evident from the high fenced pews of black oak, and the plump cushions and easy seats, deep in quaint nooks and dark recesses, that the living in that church emulated the dead. The voice of the vicar had a soft, slumberous dignity, as if he spoke through wool; one of his admirers—a poetical lady, who wrote and answered conundrums in pocket-books, and was therefore considered the literary star of Stoke-Tatlington—said, "Though she never could make out the exact words of dear Doctor Blinkinsop, yet his voice was what all dignified clergymen should imitate, it reminded her of a muffled drum!" The asthmatic little clerk was deaf—but that did not signify—for he knew exactly, as the service proceeded, how many beats would come out of the muffled drum before it was necessary for him to wheeze out "Amen!" or murmur the responses that regulated the faint hum of the congregation. Oh! that church was an incomparable place for a winter reverie, or a summer doze; never were "miserable sinners" more cosily content, never did "We beseech thee to hear us, good Lord," ooze out with more dreamy languor.

It must be confessed that some of the young people did not quite conform to the dozy decorum of the worship. The charity children played at push pin, or talked with their fingers, or "took off" the beadle as he nodded over his gold-headed stick; or, as a stock bit of fun, spoke thick in the responses, in imitation of the drumming of the vicar, or the wheezing of the clerk. Such misdoings were not confined to these restless little varlets. The young ladies were, I am sorry to say, rather given to counting the bows on each other's bonnets, and the beaux also on the men's side of the church—nor were the latter slow to reciprocate attentions. The church was, it seems, not only a good place for sleeping in, but a capital place for making assignations, carrying on small flirtations, and exhibiting new finery.

Quiet as Stoke-Tatlington called itself in modern times, there was in the days of the civil wars a strong spirit in the place; and certain Puritans who in their old-fashioned way had presumed to think the Christian life was a warfare, and not a slumber, had built a meeting-house there, for one of those ejected ministers whom the act of uniformity had driven out of the parish church. A godly man, who lived to a great age, and whose only son had perished on the field of Naseby, left a liberal endowment to the place he had so long worshipped in, and departed this life in the hope that many generations like-minded with himself might, within the humble meeting-house, have freedom to worship God according to the dictates of their conscience. And so, many good men and true had lived and preached in the house and chapel called Beulah, which, it must be owned, as little merited the name as any Zoar, or Zion, or Elim, or Ænon, which allegory run mad ever named; for pleasant or beautiful (Beulah) it certainly was not in any sense;—substantial, commodious, comfortable, it was, in spite of ugliness. But in process of time the lethargy of the parish church spread to the meeting-house. If the two did not respond in doctrine, they certainly echoed each other's snore. The Rev. Seth Settledown was a very gentlemanly man, and prided himself on being always on good terms with Dr. Blinkinsop, while the latter blandly patronised the Beulah minister by saying, " poor Settledown was better than his party—a most respectable man. And as he supposed there would be dissenters in the town, why it was well that a quiet, easy-going, decent man, he could tolerate, was the minister." Now, by this toleration, the good doctor stood well with all parties. "How liberal!" "what toleration!" "quite a man of the age!" "Think, and let think," said everybody, except an upstart bookseller, a new comer in the town, who presumed to remark, that "as to think and let think, there was not much thinking on either side."

Now, while the genteel population of Stoke-Tatlington nodded in church and dozed in chapel, the evangelical people waking up to take an interest in dinner parties, and the highly orthodox to add to that interest by some capital game at whist of winter evenings in the vicar's chosen circles, and all went smoothly on, as if eating and drinking, shuffling and cutting, and getting the odd trick, were the be-all and end-all of life, some annoyances arose which showed that, quiet as was the surface at Stoke-Tatlington, there was a rumbling and seething below rather ominous. Certain inspectors of schools, who had visited the place, reported (very impertinent of them, doubtless) that the whole juvenile population of this quiet, genteel town, were utterly ignorant. Resident tradespeople complained that the poor-rates were higher than in any place they ever lived in. The judges on circuit had remarked that the proportion of criminals to the whole population was greater than in any town in any merely agricultural district of England. That same before-mentioned bookseller had actually made a list of all the public-houses, and compared their numbers with the sellers of articles of necessary consumption—of wholesome food. He also, busy meddler that he was! took count of the commitments for drunkenness, and his tiresome paper being shown to the inspectors of schools, was taken to London, and incorporated in an article in the *Statistical Journal*, whereby it appeared from facts and figures that the tippling, the domestic brawls, and the poverty of the poor, of this exceedingly genteel town, was a something unexcelled, if not unequalled. To crown the whole, just at that unlucky time there were government investigations about paupers, and it was found that no place in England, in proportion to its population, had more children born without a legal right to their father's name than Stoke-Tatlington.

Now, just as people who live in bad air can endure odours that would choke or nauseate any one coming freshly into it, so both Dr. Blinkinsop and the Rev. Seth Settledown were quite satisfied with things as they were, thought these inquiries very impertinent, very immoral indeed, as "tending to weaken the faith of the people in their spiritual guides and teachers, and make them lean to Acts of Parliament, or educational nostrums, or some kind of moral quackery equally new and dangerous."

The rosy Doctor and his cosy dissenting brother, whom he tolerated so kindly, were drawn together more closely by what they considered the unwarrantable interference, and persecuting, meddlesome spirit of the age. They smoked their pipes together, and aided their deliberations by some choice port, and shook their heads, and nodded, and looked wise, and assented to each other in a beautifully tranquil style; but as to arriving at any conclusion, the only approach they made to demonstration was, that smoking made them thirsty, and wine was very comforting, and that leaving people alone was the duty of a free government. The vicar, to be sure, came out rather strong, for he actually quoted Scripture—not liking to be for ever outdone in that department by the Beulah minister—"Behold how good and pleasant it is for brethren to dwell together in unity," said he, as he mixed the parting glass of "something stiff," and then waxing still more eloquent—he drummed out in his muffled tones—"It needs must be that offences will come." "To be sure, my dear sir! to be sure! Very true, indeed; and what remedy is there for human depravity?" drawled out the Rev. Seth. "'Whom He will, He hardeneth;' but I beg pardon. Ahem! I did not mean to touch on doctrines."

And so these guides of the people often met and parted, mutually edified, they said. And that there was some glowing illumination from the encounter, their noses honestly testified.

Meanwhile the bookseller before named—Daniel Thorough-grain—became still more unmanageable. There was a strong endeavour to starve him out of the town, but, somehow, his shop was so well stocked, his library so good and varied, his customers so promptly and punctually served—if a periodical, or paper, or new work were wanted, he was sure to have it before the other old dreamer of a bookseller had ever heard of it—that people pocketed their dislike to the man in consideration of the advantages derived from his shop—and it was found impossible to starve him out of Stoke-Tatlington. Then, to be sure, for a long time he had, being a single man, a strong party of ladies who stood bravely by him; in the way of patronising the fancy stationery department of his shop, it must be confessed that this party flagged, and nearly deserted him, when it was discovered that he was engaged and about to be—married! but they forgave him at length, on consideration that he could after all only have selected one out of the belles of Stoke-Tatlington, and that as his bride elect was a London lady and a total stranger, he had not wounded the feelings of any of the fair residents by an invidious selection from among *them*. Then when at length he brought home his bride, she had not beauty enough to arouse envy, and she had what all could feel, as well as see, most kindly agreeable manners, and moreover possessed (an invaluable gift in a dull country town!) quite a genius for fancy work of all descriptions—aye, and nondescript, as well. So a Berlin-wool department being added to the business, Daniel Thoroughgrain was more popular than ever with his fair customers, and flourished in spite of all his foes.

He established a book club, and, as the town council would not help in it or hear of it, built a reading-room at the back of his own premises, and there he tried a winter course of lectures, and established classes for the young men of the town, which proved very successful. The landlord of "The Fox and Frying Pan," said, "That confounded fellow had

turned all the young men's brains, and that his best parlour wa
deserted by all but the old folks, who, though they sti
came, found it dull, and grumbled." The hostess of "Th
Friend at Hand," who had buried three husbands, and wa
still, while in the prime of life, adjusting the most tender an
taking widow's cap that ever aroused masculine sympathy
murmured that "if the vicar allowed such goings on, sh
was sure the church was in danger;" and when, to crow
the whole, a lecturer came who denounced the traffic in, an
the use of strong drink, and induced some fifty young me
to believe they could exist without these beverages, whic
the landlady said, "was as nat'ral as mother's milk to a
born at Stoke-Tatlington," there was such a shout abou
revolution, infidelity, chartism, that both Dr. Blinkinsop an
the Rev. Seth said, fully forty times in one evening, i
the intervals of their puffing, "Something must be done.
"Yes! something, but what?" Ah! the answer to tha
question has been the puzzle in trying times of court;
cabinets, armies, and kingdoms, and generally with the sam
result: when they come to the vague "something!" the
generally end in the blank—"nothing." But let us d
justice to both church and chapel at Stoke-Tatlingtor
"I've worn myself out in the service of—of my master,
said the reverend Beulah pastor, pulling the decanter toward
him, and pouring out a glass, "and I'm unequal to th
labour: I'll have an assistant."

"A very good thought, Sir; very good indeed. Ou
church—a venerable structure, very venerable—is, howeve;
damp. I've rheumatism, Sir, in every joint with the dam
of that place; and if I did'nt ride—and sometimes, just fc
my health—nothing more, join the hounds, Sir! I shoul
have been crippled—yes, crippled, long ago. So I mear
Sir, to have a curate. Not but I like doing duty: I've bee
a working clergyman, Sir, and my flock liked my voic
until that upsetting fellow, Thoroughgrain, came her
Why, Sir, I never even married! because I wished to elevat
myself to———"

"Does'nt that—ahem! Pardon me, dear Doctor! bu
does'nt that a little, just a little, savour of Romanism; bu
I don't want to be personal or doctrinal. I've been, as yo

know, the husband of two wives, both exemplary women, though I rather apprehend they both worked themselves to death; for there's so much expected with us of a minister's wife, that if she have a proper care of her husband's health, and undertakes visiting the people, to spare him, and super-intending the Sunday school, and having a Bible class, or a Dorcas, or some such thing,—why, these added to her home duties generally, do require an amount of—of energy, that few women, however gifted, can exert."

This long speech was, we are sorry to say, lost on the Doctor, who was nodding in his chair; and so the Rev. Seth returned to his dwelling, and wrote to the Principal of——— college, stating his want of an assistant; and for some weeks there was a little pleasant excitement in both church and chapel, canvassing the merits of the curate and the assistant on trial in their respective places of worship.

Dr. Blinkinsop was not easily pleased, for he had been so long used to his own muffled tones, as he boomed out the prayers, that the reading of the curates annoyed him, as it well might. What, with some intoning, and others gabbling, he barely recognized the prayers, but he wanted a sonorous indistinct monotony, and that he could not get. Then, when he heard the sermon praised by the church-warden, who had most intelligence, the good Doctor thought it right to say to the young man, "I hope you're not anxious about preaching. That's the heresy of the dissenters. They go to hear fine sermons:—though Settledown, worthy man! never spoilt his people much in that way."

Equally perplexed was the Beulah pastor, though he had a greater choice to select from. He parted in a huff with two young men because they visited the people, and with another because he was eloquent. "Don't be hunting for popularity, it's the vice of our age," said he. But as many of the young people of both church and chapel were members of Thorough-grain's book club, and attended the lectures and classes, it happened that at length there were two young men each of whom was so highly popular in their respective places, that the elders, tired of fault-finding, and wanting that quiet which is so needful to the discussion of, not politics or theo-logy, but wines and spirits, with great dignity withdrew opposition, and left a fair field to the new comers, content, the one with the endowment and the other with the tithes, to permit others to do the work.

Mr. Carey Pierce, the Beulah assistant, was certainly an original; for he was very fortunately free from that particular stomach complaint that Timothy had, and that Paul prescribed for. He was assuredly remarkable in this respect, for every one knows Timothy's ailment is as common a ministerial affliction in our day, as if the dissenting teachers, in rivalry of the spiritual claims of others to apostolical succession, set up for being the actual bodily descendants of Timothy. And as to the remedy, " Take a little wine for thy stomach's sake," why it is stereotyped on almost every brain among them. While Paul's other prescription, " It is good neither to eat flesh nor drink wine, nor anything by which thy brother stumbleth, or is offended, or is made weak," is nearly forgotten,—or at all events, is folded away in that unvisited nook of memory, where repose the words, " If thy right eye or hand offend thee, pluck it out—cut it off,"—or " Take up thy cross and follow me," and other such unpopular and unpalatable directions.

It certainly astonished the easy-going folks of Stoke-Tatlington to find that Carey Pierce, though he could not find time to visit their dinner parties or evening amusements, contrived to have a Christian instruction society for the young people, a maternal meeting for the matrons, adult evening classes for those who had grown up in ignorance (and they were many) of reading and writing, a day school for the children, as well as a complete revival of the Sunday school, and a Temperance society for the general public. He divided the town into districts, raised an army of volunteers to distribute tracts and make themselves acquainted with the condition of the poor; he had a special service for working people who had hitherto shrunk not only from the gospel, but from the satin and broad-cloth that had so palpably said, " Stand off, I am holier than thou ;" and by getting these neglected ones habituated to the assembling of themselves together, they were gradually coming to strive after such decency of apparel as enabled them, without offence to others or themselves, to mingle in the Sabbath services.

Now, this activity was contagious.   The kind and good young curate, Mr. Retriever, it is true, was not used to such rapid doings, nor was he permitted to establish exactly such machinery as Carey Pierce set agoing.   But he was roused; and being as earnest a Churchman as the other was a Dissenter, they emulated each other in a noble rivalry.   Mr. Retriever had some advantages of social position; he was, of what is called a good family, and could command the wealth of others, if he had none of his own: so he resolved to have the dwellings of the poor improved.   He busied himself on sanitary matters.   The Health of Town's Commissioners found an ally in him when the Stoke-Tatlington Town Council insisted that their town needed no drainage; and by his exertions, the " Muckabites," as the dirt lovers were called, were worsted.   Then he collected a good sum for baths and wash-houses, and was even brave enough, in the teeth of the whole medical profession, to give a lecture at Thoroughgrain's Room, on the "Rationale of Health and Disease."   He attended the meetings of the guardians of the poor, and was moreover, often at the workhouse and the prison, and as he inquired diligently into the causes of poverty and crime, it unfolded itself clearly before him that the tavern was the tempting vestibule that led to the cell of the criminal, and the ward of the workhouse, and not unfrequently the strait waistcoat of the lunatic, and the sick-bed of the infirmary. Under this impression he attended the quarter sessions, and proved such facts to the board of magistrates as compelled them to refuse some licences and suspend others, so that " *the* trade," as it is emphatically called, (as though it ought to take precedence of all others) was most terribly shaken, and many shifted their quarters, saying, " Stoke-Tatlington was ruined; no publican could live there."   Moreover, a railway was in progress, and the young clergyman established plans to meet that well-paid but almost barbarian class—the excavators; and when those rude athletes left the district, many of them had to take a handsome sum out of the savings bank, instead of returning paupers to their own parishes.

Do not suppose, O reader, that these two young reformers had not their trials and temptations.   Sometimes they were checked by well meant but timid cautions—" Oh! you're going too fast and too far." Sometimes they were misrepresented by prejudice—"Oh! both Retriever and Pierce have their own ends to gain." Then the ladies, dear hearts, "even their failings lean to virtue's side," (and I hate to pen the record), they tried by flattery, coaxing, pressing invitations —genteel excuses for a little wine-bibbing—"just a little after all the fatigues," to put on them that instrument—with which women have often quenched the light they meant to conserve—an extinguisher.

But there was an earnestness of purpose about both these young men that put to flight, as with a mighty rushing wind, all feather-brains. Silly women, it might be, came at first to hear the new curate, or the new assistant minister, and as both were single men, might (such is human weakness) speculate on probabilities ; but they either remained to think of something very different, or they came no more. There was neither time nor inclination for either small talk or dangling after ladies, or being the oracle of tea tables. Miss Althea Fluff, the poetess, who so loved the voice of Dr. Blinkinsop, and for thirty years had sweetly composed herself to sleep in the parish church under the influence of the "muffled drum," used to declare that " she was glad she was not doomed to be a young woman in such degenerate days as these, for the young men of the present time were not fit to hold a candle to Dr. Blinkinsop, whose only fault (dear, good, man !) was, that he took a long time to make up his mind." " Ah ! yes," she would say, looking in her glass with a sigh, "procrastination is the thief of time." Perhaps the secret of the activity of both the young ministers was, that they felt they were accountable to a higher tribunal than public opinion. The eternal verities had struck home to their hearts, " Ye are bought with a price ;" " One is your master, even Christ, and all ye are brethren." "Forasmuch as ye did it unto one of the least of these, ye did it unto me." These and a hundred similar truths had entered not merely the recesses of their ears, but vibrated through the inmost recesses of their being, prompting the entire consecration of themselves to the glory of God and the good of men. How, with such thoughts within them, and such work around them, could they linger and trifle? They would not, they dared not.

It was seen and felt that these were men, not effigies and formulas, and machines, — real, living, thinking, working men, intent upon "their master's business;" and before them all that was false and hollow fled, unable to abide their presence.   True, it could no longer be said that the church and chapel parsons smoked and hobnobbed lovingly together, — the days of such good fellowship were certainly over, but somehow there was a cordiality of respect when the young rival reformers met, either in street or on platform, which had never been before observed.   It was not condescension and servility, with a little qualmish misgiving on both sides, but real, manly, hearty esteem and friendship.   In argument on doctrines, and discipline, on Church or State, they certainly never did, and never would agree ; but they agreed in doing all the good they could, and the town reaped the benefit.   And though heads, as it were, of different households, they each walked before their households with a perfect heart.   Mind the words, "walked before," they did not stand and point the way the others should go, and never took a step themselves ; nor did they lag after them, or reluctantly follow afar off ; they walked before—

"Allured to brighter worlds, and led the way.'

Meanwhile, whatever publicans might testify, trade was brisk in Stoke-Tatlington.   Drapers and clothiers, and butchers and bakers, as well as our friend the bookseller, all were exemplifying the maxim, "Strive and thrive."   Builders were mighty busy pulling down and beautifying ; and what with new shop fronts, and a handsome town hall, and new schools where the cage and stocks used to stand, the High Street was, as the parish clerk said, (he loved long words,) "transmogrified into metropolitan granjer."   The poor-rates were lower by more than a half, and the worst drunkard in the place had turned tee-totaler.   It must be owned that some old ladies insisted on it, that the gentility of the town was gone.   "When maps are hung up in common schools, and poor children learn drawing, there's an end of course to social distinctions," said Miss Althea Fluff, at a whist table, —the only family, by the way, where card parties were continued, and where poor Dr. Blinkinsop could still chuckle

over the odd trick! While health came on the wing of
the tempest that had so changed Stoke-Tatlington, how did
the stately old Doctor, and the worthy ancient minister, bear
the shaking and uprooting of much that time had rendered
not only endurable but pleasant to them? Oh! they were
not so much disturbed by the upsetting times as many
people supposed. They each held fast of a strong rope that
steadied them, and kept them from being swept away,
namely, the emoluments of the vicarage, and the endowment of the chapel. Neither the vicar nor the pastor could
be displaced, and though they must have had a dim consciousness that they were not exactly useful in either place,
yet they considered themselves ornamental. The vicar took
out and aired several of his choice purchased manuscript
sermons, congratulating himself that as he never preached a
page of his own writing, he was the less responsible for the
matter; but when he found the church quite deserted at the
time he preached, except by his fair poetical friend, he gave
it up, and took an extra glass of negus as a consolation for
the want of taste and gratitude that characterised his people.
The Rev. Seth Settledown was not all at once quite so
quiescent, he determined to preach doctrine, and put down
this spirit of work-mongering; but whether they were high
and dry, or deep and dull, or whatever was the fault of his
sermons, no mortal man, woman, or child—no, not even the
Rev. gentleman himself—could make any thing clearly out.
It was a fog; and he floundered and groped about dismally.
Some one said it reminded them of unrolling a mummy,—
there were long tedious bandages—dusty and dark—untwin-
ing and untwisting, until, when your patience was quite
worn out, you came at length to a frame of dry bones, and
an exhalation of dust that choked you.

So in sheer self-defence the good people of Beulah agreed,
on condition that he did not insist on preaching, to give up
the endowment to the Rev. Seth for his life; and they volun-
teered to maintain their young minister, and the various
benevolent institutions of the place, independent of any
endowment whatever. And they kept their word.

And so the old vicar and the old minister hung on to life.
The former paralysed for many years, and wheeled about on

fine days in a Bath chair, walking beside which might be seen Miss Althea Fluff, who, with more poetry of feeling than she had ever had of expression, was faithful to the last in her admiration of the "muffled drum;" and when at length suddenly the pipe dropped out of the old man's mouth, and gave notice by its fall on the floor that he was dead, she wept real tears and said, " She never should hear such a voice again."

But poor Seth had a severer trial,—an agonizing internal malady that long had threatened, set in upon him with desperate strength ; and the conviction came, too late—at least as far as this world is concerned—that his costly comforting beverages had been laying up " wrath against the day of wrath." As the poor body writhed in intolerable torture, he often said to his doctors, " Why did'nt you tell me I was wrong in my diet? What's the use of your skill, if it only judges results and does not foresee them." As the frame wore away in the fierce strife, the mind became clearer. Life ! duty ! assumed a different aspect. The light of eternity came lurid, yet distinct into the dark valley, and gave a spectral glare to the shadows of death. " Woe is me! woe is me!" said the appalled and trembling sinner ! " Oh! if I was but raised up again, how differently would I live, how earnestly would I labour! woe is me!" In vain did Carey Pierce endeavour to soothe him, and watched beside him, and prayed with him : he wailed and lamented, and would not be comforted, still muttering as the stupor of coming dissolution filmed his eyes, and weighed down his eyelids, "Woe is me!" He did, however, pause in that cry, as Carey repeated aloud the words " I will arise and go to my father, and say unto him, Father, I have sinned, and am no more worthy to be called thy son." It was evident to all that the ear of the dying man took in the sense of the divine words—ay, and applied them. There was a pause, when every one held their breath, and listened for another breathing of the sufferer, and they saw the gloom depart, and a serene calm fix the rigid features ; and Carey, who knew that it was death, could not help saying, with tears, of the poor departing penitent, " And while he was yet a great way off, his Father saw him, and had compassion on him, and ran and fell on his neck, and kissed him." And even so let us quit the scene.

And now, reader, it is by no means our intention to say that perfection has found a home at Stoke-Tatlington. There's some sin, and sorrow, and poverty there—quite enough to keep good people busy, and kind people compassionate, and thoughtful people humble. But there's healthy, vigorous life there. And it is the opinion of the writer of this account, that anything is better than stagnation. There's one quality in which the good may safely imitate the bad. "Imitate the bad, in what?" In activity.

"A BIT OF A FROLIC."

"Memory like a fiend shall follow,
Night and day, the steps of crime.
SIR BULWER LYTTON.

IN the history of great crimes, there is nothing of which the
world knows so little, as of the remote, often slow, process
that leads to their commission. The public hear of some
awful deed of sin, and amid their indignation and horror,
rush to the natural and easy conclusion, that the perpetrator
of such iniquity is a monster out of the pale of humanity—
an abnormal creature, unfit to live, whose name and deed
cannot be too soon forgotten,—or, with a morbid curiosity,
the crime and its consequences are dwelt on as an excitement gratifying the appetite for the wondrous and horrible.
How seldom does the mind investigate the causes that oper-
ate to lead or hurry the criminal to the consummation of his
guilt. And yet this is the really valuable lesson, apart from
which the details of all crime and punishment must be merely
revolting and vulgar.

By no means must we accept the hasty and lazy solution
that criminals are simply monsters, whose predispositions to
special sins were not discovered or surmised, because of our
charity or our innocence, but who had doubtless the mark of
the beast on them, only our purity did not recognize it.
After the event we argue thus, and shrink from the awful
idea, that these noted sinners are men of like passions with
ourselves—"The Lord looketh from heaven: He beholdeth
all the sons of men. He fashioneth their hearts alike"
(Psalm xxxiii. 13-15) ; and therefore it is His grace that
keeps us from falling, and makes us to differ from the male-
factors whose crimes and punishments we know, whose
temptations we do not know.

The indolence of our nature notes only results.   Are there fewer "*Betters*" on the race-course, since Palmer, in the prime of his early manhood, quivered in the hangman's grasp, and his dishonoured remains were thrown as a naked heap of carrion into the prison grave?   No!   Every race-course shows sportsmen keen in their gambling, raising money how they can, mad in their excitement, staving off losses by more reckless risks,—heaping up wrath for the day of wrath.   "Palmer the poisoner," they say, "Oh, he was a monster! what is his fate to us?"   Palmer would never have been "the poisoner" if he had not been the gambler. The poor of Rugeley say—"We can't make it out no how, for he wur main kind and pleasant."

A foreign gentleman of the mildest demeanour visits a country town to give a lecture.   He is a guest in one of those happy, humble households of which Britain is so justly proud.   Little children climb his knees, look confidingly into the depths of his clear, calm, dark eyes, nestle to his bosom lovingly, as he says, "I have two little girls far away, will you kiss me for them?" and with gathering tears the children, feeling rather than understanding the sorrow of the exile, soothe him with their caresses, and are at home with him, and he with them.   While the father in that household, looking at the noble lineaments of his guest, wonders what can be the state of that country which expatriates such a son, and wonder is increased when he hears him lecture, the fire kindling in his eyes, and lighting up his countenance, till, through all impediments of our unaccustomed northern tongue, the living power of eloquence breaks forth, not loud, not fierce, but calm and thrilling, till his hearers weep for outraged liberty, and cry, "Let God arise, let his enemies be scattered."   The stranger takes his departure from that quiet town, amid the sylvan glades of merry England, and leaves behind him a memory of gentleness and sorrow. "Of all the men I ever knew," said one, who had looked upon a wide circle of human life, "I never saw a man I should deem less likely to commit violence of any kind"— assuredly not assassination—and yet, reader, that interesting stranger was Orsini!   He had nursed anger until it became hatred, cherished indignation until it degenerated into re-

venge. Ah! evil thoughts, like unclean birds, may unin-
vited flit over the head; but the sin is ours if they roost
there.

The electric telegraph was no sooner in working order between London and Windsor, than it was the means of cap-
turing a murderer. He had left his victim in her death-
agony from poison, and fled, as swift as the express could
carry him, to London; but the subtle messenger of the wires
was swifter, and the miserable man but hastened to his cap-
tors who awaited him. All Britain rang with this crime.
"Monster! fiend!" were the epithets echoed everywhere.
Meanwhile, the wife of this man, an intelligent, amiable
woman, could never be brought to believe him guilty. He,
so kind, so good! she was nursing her first son, who bore
his wretched parent's name; the mother when that name was
given, said, "I only hope he may prove as good a man as his
father." All fanciful theories of men learning goodness and
mercy from flowers and beautiful natural objects were over-
thrown here. This man's conservatory was his pride; he
lived among his flowers, and his house looked not only on a
lovely rural scene, but an old grey church tower rose before
his windows, and a little parsonage embowered in shrubs
nestled near; where one of the truest and gentlest of England's poet sons had first seen the light, his genius to every
thoughtful mind yet shedding a halo over the place.

This man had nourished sensual passions. He feared exposure. "One more crime—only one, would free him," was
the whisper of the fiend—"and his name of husband, father,
and citizen would be untarnished." He plunged into that
one crime; it was the pit of death.

About twenty years ago, there was an aged couple who
lived in a pleasant suburb of the metropolis. They had
some married daughters, and one son, the child of their old
age. Among the diligent boys at the National School of the
district, this lad, whom we will call George Smith, was the
first and foremost. He was not a handsome, nor a very
bright boy, but thoughtful, punctual, plodding; if he gained
a place in his class, he kept it by sheer industry, and was
therefore the kind of boy the schoolmaster would praise, and
parents would be proud of; for there seemed much to hope

C

from his diligence, and little to fear from the ordinary indolence or waywardness of boyhood.   The course of instruction
was but very limited at the school; but as George went
gradually and carefully up through it all, what he knew he
knew thoroughly.   His attainments seemed wonderful to his
parents, who, having been most of their lives domestic servants, belonged to perhaps one of the least intelligent of the
labouring classes.   The father, whose employment at the
time we write of was that of a waiter, at dinner and evening
parties, was doubly industrious and careful, in the hope of
putting his steady boy to a higher school, when a great
calamity befell the household—the mother was smitten with
paralysis, and though she retained her mental faculties, she
lay on her bed utterly helpless, and soon hopeless of ever
recovering, though death might be long before he opened the
door of release.   Very heavy in any home is such a visita-
tion; to the poor dwelling it is often ruin.   It is indeed a
dreadful storm on life's rough ocean, that smites the active
mother, and lays her a wreck upon the strand of time.
George and his father not only missed the hands that had
ministered to them, but they had now to tend and minister
to her, and to their honour be it said, they did their part
well and tenderly.   Smith gave up much of his work that
called him long away from home, though it was his most
profitable employment, and took such jobs as lay near at
hand, and did not require him long to leave the invalid.   The
boy forgot all pride of sex, and turned his hand to housework, with a ready skill, that comforted his mother's heart,
as she watched him from her bed with loving eyes, and murmured her tremulous blessings on his filial care.   The writer
is thrilled with awe at the remembrance of the many prayers
put up from that humble room for George.   What tears,
too, were shed by the mother, that no more schooling could
be afforded for him who had so profited by his humble op-
portunities. Tract distributors, and sick-visitors who entered
that home, decent in its lowliness, and sacred in its sorrows,
would often quit the scene with moistened eyes, and humble
hearts, saying, with undoubting faith, " He hath chosen the
poor of this world, rich in faith, and heirs of the kingdom."
    As George could not pursue the plan the father had wished

him, and must, of course, earn his bread, he became an errand boy at a stationer's shop in the neighbourhood; and the pleasure of taking home his

"Sair won penny-fee,"

was so sweet, that all sorrow about the check to his educational advancement passed easily from the elastic mind of youth. From a dark, thoughtful boy, he grew rapidly into a stout, ruddy youth, while in his new occupation; his father, meanwhile, lamenting that some pursuit more suited to his son's advancing years did not open for him. At length, a clergyman, who had, with interest, watched the boy's career at his school and home, procured him a situation in a gentleman's family, as junior servant, or "page," as it is the fashion to call servant boys.

The American citizen may survey a livery with scorn, particularly if he believes that nature has clothed the serving class in a ready-made livery of black; and there is certainly to the philosopher nothing very dignified in the plush and gold, the tags and frippery of flunkeydom; but, nevertheless, young George, in his well-fitting dark suit and bright buttons, looked splendid in his poor mother's eyes, as he stood by her bedside, and said, "Now, mother, I shall get on, and you'll see how I'll save, and try to help you."

"Be a good servant, and never mind me, my boy. I shall do well enough," was the sick mother's cheery answer.

"Aye, aye; mind what your mother says, George," was the brief advice of the father—a man inclined to be silent, and whose dark face, though mild and calm, seldom was lighted with a smile. Never servant lad went with better recommendations, intentions, or prospects, into a virtuous household, than did young George Smith. Twice a-week, for half-an-hour, while the family were in town, he was to visit his parents—their home being in a small house at the rear of —— Place, where George's master lived.

"A virtuous household," we said. Yes; so far as the heads of the family and their children, and the rules by which they regulated their dwelling were concerned. But under the surface, who can tell the evil that may be lurking, like volcanic forces far below some verdant, smiling plain. A

gentleman and lady, and their two grown-up daughters were
the family. A lady's-maid, cook, two housemaids, butler,
and page, were the attendants. And a well-ordered group
they seemed; regular as clockwork went the house—prayers,
and meals, and church-going; eating, working, visiting, sleeping—all exact, orderly, respectable. There was, however, a
feud between the lady's-maid and cook. Both being important functionaries, they were outwardly civil and inwardly
jealous of each other, like functionaries in a higher servitude.
The lady's-maid was an old but stern—a good but severe
woman—who had imitated the reserve of aristocratic manners
until she was like an ice-berg, and her really respectable
character exerted no influence for good on the younger servants. She was a Christian in faith and practice, but she
did not recommend Christianity. The cook, Mrs. Touter,
was a widow, obsequious, shrewd, active; a clever servant,
seen from the employer's point of sight; indulgent, jovial,
sensual, and popular, in aspects known only to intimates.
The butler and upper housemaid were ordinary specimens of
their class, with whom our story has nothing to do. The
under housemaid, Anne, was a young, pretty, country girl,
the niece to Mrs. Abby, the lady's-maid. It was the first
situation Anne had filled, and her aunt looked sharply after
her, and took care that when the housework was done, the
girl should have plenty of needle-work to fill up her time.
But Anne needed no looking after. She was a conscientious,
good girl, well brought up in her far-off country-home. She
brought a conscience as open and clear as her fair young
face, to her London dwelling and duties. Touter would have
liked this girl, but as a relation of Abby's she chose to consider
her a spy; and it was quite in the nature of a woman who
loved scandal, and had lived most of her life in places where
it was rife, to disbelieve Anne's relationship of niece to Abby,
and to insinuate where she could, that there was a nearer and
less lawful tie between them. Touter was the only one among
the servants who took or loved the drunkard's drink. She often
complained that she never lived with such a hum-drum set; but
yet, amid all her faults, her merriment, and her comfortable
way of catering for the servant's table, made her a favourite.
No fiend is so dangerous as the one who comes with a laugh

Laughter unlocks the door of the heart. George's home had been saddened by his mother's illness; he yielded at once to Touter's good-humour, never inquiring how much was genuine and trust-worthy, and how much came bottled from the wine-vaults. And he was not alone; Anne would innocently laugh at jokes she did not fully understand, just because they sounded funny, and wished her Aunt Abby was not so crabbed, like a cloud upon the place. Never was Touter in such high glee as when Abby had scolded her niece; never did she try so much to ingratiate herself with Anne as at such times. Months passed on, George was growing into manhood; and it did not escape the keen eyes of Touter that the youth was ever ready to lend a helping hand to lighten any of Anne's toils. With the coarseness of a sensual nature, she joked the young people, and turned their thoughts, perhaps already so disposed, into the dangerous channel of the affections. Anne, modest and prudent, took fright at her words, and wisely put herself more than ever under her aunt's eye. George seemed possessed by a new nature— restless, watching, fitful. Touter's jokes filled him strangely both with laughter and loathing. The woman saw her power over the youth, saw his weakness, and resolved to make him the means of mortifying her enemy, Abby, in the person of her niece.

It happened, most unfortunately, that the family rather suddenly left town. They took with them the butler and Abby, and the housemaid, leaving Touter in charge of the house, and the two youngest servants. Abby had made her niece a good needle-woman, and a stock of work was left for Anne to complete in the absence of the family. No sooner was the house in —— Place, left to Touter's charge, than she began in jovial mood to say she would take care the youngsters had a merry time of it. But Anne coldly repulsed her advances, and began, on the first day, as she continued, to work upstairs in her Aunt Abby's room, as she had been desired to do. Indignant at the girl's decision, Touter veiled her anger with a show of great friendship for George, was full of sympathising inquiries for his mother, and gradually introduced her ally—the ally of every villany—strong drink. She had cunning enough to see that unaided by this ally she would be powerless. Teetotalism had not then entered that district; within two years from that time, there was a flourishing society in that neighbourhood, but then the true character of the inflaming, insidious, maddening draught was unknown, except in its most coarse and obvious results. Touter knew—a knowledge not uncommon now, any more than then, among servants—how to drink largely without being a drunkard. How to administer the bewitching draught cautiously, enough to inflame—"elevate" she called it—and not to stupify. But Anne's innocence was an impenetrable shield. Her country rearing and simple tastes made strong drink unpleasant to her. "No, Touter! you are very kind, but I dislike it, indeed I do," was her answer to every invitation; there was no getting her to yield. George, brought up in London, and fully believing "a little drop of something short," one of the blessings of life, yielded to Touter's wish, and, to use her words, "knew how to make himself comfortable like a sensible fellow." Always as Touter and George hob-nobbed together, Anne was the subject of conversation. The poor youth's hopes and fears, his love and jealousy, how she played on them. A bad woman needs no education to teach her craft, she has it by nature. One evening, George, under the influence of this demon's whisperings, and drams, threw off the decent reserve he had always hitherto shown, and jumping up at the supper table, attempted some boisterous romping with Anne, who, thoroughly hurt and indignant, repelled him with sharp scorn, and rushed to the shelter of her room. Whenever people are in fault, they are sure to be angry; and George, stung by the repulse, was in a flame of rage. Touter added to it by taunts, saying, "Oh, you're afraid of madam's airs." "She only does that to try you;" "she's not really offended—not she," and similar sly bits of taunt. Fevered and wretched, the youth went to his bed, every evil passion inflamed, all good desires put to flight. In the morning, his tempter began her taunts and jeers again. "What! cast down at a girl's tricks; she only wanted you to follow her." "See the bright ribbon my lady has on her collar to-day, that's to make up last night's quarrel." "You're only a milk-sop of a boy, get that ribbon, and I'll call you a man, and so will she."

"I will get it," said George, unhallowed fires kindling in his dark eyes.

"Not you; I'll wager all the money I have."

"I will," he reiterated.

"No, no; not you!"

This banter—infamy to the woman—madness to the youth, went on, until his mind was on fire with evil. Touter brought out her bottle and glass, poured out a dram and drank, "Here's to your success, lad, which I'll believe when I see the ribbon." Then giving a glass to George, the infatuated youth said, "You shall believe it; I'll get it before I am two hours older." Just then Touter put on her bonnet and shawl, and said, "I'm going out a bit, to call on a friend of mine; I may stay till dusk, but I shan't be late;" and with a hideous leer in her eyes, and a foul jest on her tongue, away she went.

Like a serpent coiling round the branches of a tree, the thought of that ribbon coiled and wound round every feeling of the wretched lad's mind. Stealthily he crept up stairs. Anne was writing a letter (it proved to be a letter of complaint to her aunt at being left in town). He caught a side view of her; the ribbon, as she stooped, touched the paper; he made a spring towards her; with a half-scream she rose, when the door bell rung twice loudly, and habit prevailing over passion, George ran down and opened the door—it was the postman. According to custom he took the letters to the butler's room, and in his hurry opened the drawer above that in which the letters were usually deposited. What demon at his side had made his hand stumble on the wrong drawer? What sight was it, that, as he threw the letters in with feverish haste, arrested his attention? A razor! a half-open razor! left there by the careless butler. He seized it madly. Was it to frighten her? Was it to shear the ribbon from her neck? He said so, said it in a penitent, dying hour. Alas! in five minutes from that time, he had rushed up stairs; there had been a scuffle; a struggle from that upper-room all down the blood-stained staircase to the drawing-room, and there fell the poor victim, weltering in her blood, dead, hideously murdered!

Out of the house, hunted by ten thousand fiends, fled the

miserable wretch.   Up into the Fulham Road, away to the
fields, on he went, his dress as a servant, making his swift-
ness seem that of a messenger; many looked after but none
stopped or questioned him, as he went on—on, in a blind,
agonised haste, he knew not whither.   Meanwhile, as the
golden twilight of the summer's evening deepened into night,
the greater criminal returned, and was standing on the steps
under the mild beams of the newly risen moon, knocking and
ringing at the door. If, at first, sensual thoughts came into the
grovelling mind of the dram-drinker, as she waited to be let in
by her victims, they were soon driven away by fright, when
she could get no admission.   The servant next door, roused by
the ringing, came out, but could give no information.   She
had seen no one go out.   She remembered the postman had
called; for she had been watching his coming on her own
account.   Touter, unwilling to speak to the police, asked
to be allowed to go into the back garden of this house, and
by climbing over the wall she entered her master's safely—
none of the back doors or windows, to her marvel, being
closed.   It looked dark and eerie as she entered, after the
bright streets and the calm moonlight.   She shouted
"George!" "Anne!" and too excited to wait to kindle a
lamp, she went calling up the house to Anne's work-room;
she kicked against an inkstand on the floor, picked up a piece
of paper, the half-written letter; but without thinking much
of this, returned down stairs, and entering the drawing-room,
was crossing to pull down the blinds, when her foot slipped,
and she stumbled over—what?   The scream that rang
through the house was heard by the servants next door—
was heard by the policeman on his beat—was heard by
passing wayfarers, who shuddered at its import, and involuntarily took up the cry, adding the word, "Murder!"
"murder!!"

Hurrying feet entered that dwelling; men used to scenes
of violence gathered in that drawing-room, and stood horror-
stricken at the sight awaiting them.   Lying on her side; her
pallid face looking, in the moonlight, calm and pure as
marble; her long hair loosed from its fastenings, falling over
throat and bosom, and hiding the ghastly wound that had
supplied the pool of gore, from which they shudderingly

recoiled, while an outstretched, open hand, stiffened in its impotent defence, seemed now as if raised in mute appeal to Heaven. A stony silence fell upon the first beholders, broken only by others coming with lights, and by the loud screams, on the stairs, of the wretched woman who had prompted the deed, but who dared not again enter that chamber of death, and behold her work. With hushed voices and reverential tread, the police drew down the blinds, and shut out the tranquil moonlight. A neighbour, known as a confidential friend of the family, speedily came; a sheet was spread over the dead, the uplifted hand raising it like a canopy; and then began the search for the murderer. The house, the neighbouring roofs and gardens were all searched in vain that night. The next morning was Sunday. In these days of electric telegraphs, the master of the dwelling could be instantly apprised of such a tragedy; how tardy then was the swiftest process! The morning mail took the before-mentioned neighbour out of town to the country sojourn of his friend, to convey the tidings. The night mail brought back the head of the house to his desecrated dwelling. As yet the murderer had not been captured; but, before the world, awakening to its Monday's toil with freshened energies, had begun to circulate a hue-and-cry, or offer a reward, the guilty youth was in the hands of justice. Thirty-six hours he had wandered, foodless and shelterless, in the fields and villages that skirt the western side of the metropolis; if he had lain down it had been in some ditch, wishing, in his despair, to die. Foot-sore, worn, haggard, he had, at length, sought his doom and given himself up to justice.

No need to tell the details of the trial; all was plain, as to the deed and the doer; the verdict and doom were—GUILTY —DEATH. But the chief criminal, the instigator, whose fiery drams, and whose foul hints inflamed the brain, and nerved the felon hand, escaped with a reprimand for leaving the house, and went whimpering out of court, with the words, "It was only a joke—a bit of a frolic." Early, on a fine morning, in the week following the murder, the remains of poor Anne were consigned to their last resting-place, her old father and mother following, and people weeping as they saw the two grey heads bending over the untimely grave of their young daughter—all hearts throbbing for them with yearning sympathy.

But there was another, and a far sadder scene. The little room where George's bed-ridden mother lay; and her husband sat stupified, making no reply to her questions. "Where's my George?" "Is he ill?" "What's the matter?" The good clergyman of the district; the benevolent doctor who attended her, met in that room, but hesitated how to tell her. They felt it would be present death, word it as carefully as they might. But she must be told; for street newsmen were bawling the "——— Place tragedy" through all the streets; they came into that where the wretched parents lived. The father, at the hateful sound, rushed to a back attic of the house, locked himself in, and was heard rolling on the floor in his bitter agony. Poor neighbours gathered their little pittance, and gave it to these hawkers, only to increase the nuisance; for as soon as they heard that the parents lived there, these vultures came in troops, spent the pence given in charity at the neighbouring gin-shop, and, stimulated with the hardihood of gin and brutality of beer, bawled their dismal tidings all the louder, until the tradespeople of the district formed themselves into a troop, at each end of the street, and kept the ruffians out.

The tale is told. The youth died penitent for his crime. The mother never fully comprehended the matter, and, in a few weeks, ceased to call for her boy—the youngling of her flock, the staff of her age. To a neighbour, who called one evening, she spoke with sudden animation, saying, "I'm much better; I mean to go to-morrow and find out the truth about our poor boy;" and it was a relief to find her words fulfilled— she went out next day from shams and shadows, through the gate of death to the realm of truth.

For some years, a dark, silent old man used to wander listlessly about the lanes of Brompton, and the pleasant fields and gardens of Fulham, very harmless and very taciturn. His simple wants were provided for by the hand of benevolence. They said he was insane, for he could never be got to answer any question, or to converse with any one. Sometimes he muttered a few words, but all that could be gathered from them was, "She said it was 'a joke!'" "She called it 'a bit of frolic!'" Poor, old wanderer! Rest came at last. Better a grief like thine than the career of drunkenness and infamy of thy son's betrayer—beginning in the dram-glass, ending in the blackness of darkness for ever and ever.

KEEPING A CONSCIENCE.

A NIGHT SCENE.

" How happy is he born and taught,
  That serveth not another's will;
Whose armour is his honest thought,
  And simple truth his utmost skill."
                SIR HENRY NOTTON.

IT was a rough winter night. The wind, in long heavy blasts, swept a wild, moorland tract in the north of England, and rushed down upon a little town that lay just over the edge of the moor, with a fury that soon cleared the steep, ill-paved streets of all passengers but such as were compelled to face its rage. The sign-boards of the various public-houses creaked as they swung threateningly over the causeway, and here and there banging doors, and the loud barking of defiant dogs, filled the momentary lull of the wind, that seemed to sink and swell like billows round the houses. But from many a window came a gleam of light that told of bright firesides and cozy rooms, where the howling of the wind without only increased the sense of comfort within. A solitary horseman rode at a brisk trot over the moor—his sure-footed steed evidently accustomed both to rough riding and rough roads. The traveller is expected; for at the bow-window of a lonely house on the outskirts of the town a lady is holding back the curtain, and looking over the paddock in front, towards the wild path that leads from the wilder moors. How lovely the slender form at the window looks, standing in the crimson gleam reflected from a bright fire, and lamp, shedding their rays on the red curtain which her white hand holds aside with such unconscious grace! No wonder that the horseman reins up a moment before he approaches the friendly gate, and, wild as the night is, feasts his eyes on the charming picture that stands, in all its nymph-like grace, clearly defined before him. But the curtain is hastily dropped, and in a moment after the outer door has opened, and a voice, distinct in its bell-like clearness, even amid the roaring of the blast, calls, "Walter! dear Walter! why do you not make haste? Here, Tom; here's your master—be quick! How it blows!"

"Yes, rebel," said the horseman, as he leaped down: "and why could you not stay patiently within, like a wise woman, you little feather-brain."

"No such thing, Walter. If I were feather-brain, I should be blown away to-night, instead of which here I am."

As this was said, there was a little leap forward, into arms that, sooth to say, seemed to expect the burden, and to bear it into the house gaily enough.

"Is this the way, Mistress Jessy, you receive your tired husband, and lighten his toils, saucy helpmate that you are —helpless, I think I must say."

"Helpless! Say such a word, if you dare, in the presence of this bright fire. This kettle, Sir, sings a loud denial from the hob, and the toast and tea are warm in their defence of your helpful wife. Your very slippers are ready to fly in your face at such an aspersion."

As the little, laughing wife uttered these words, her busy hands were arranging the tea-table; while Walter, as she called him, was throwing off his cloak, and preparing to do honour to the comfortable evening meal.

Yes! comfortable—that was the word for the meal and the room. It was very plainly furnished—a round centre-table, a few cane chairs, a well-stocked book-case, full crimson curtains, now drawn closely over the one wide window, and a hearth, whose bright fender and irons multiplied the dancing light of the glowing fire, and gleamed over the neat, checked carpet. A work basket on a side table, two vases filled with wax flowers, under glass shades, on the mantle-piece, told of woman's hand and taste. Some fine Crayon drawings were the only decoration of the walls, except the certificate of a surgeon, that, framed and glazed, occupied a recess by the fire-place. How many rooms, all gilding and glitter, French polish and drapery, looked less pleasant and *home*-like, than this little parlour! Cleanliness and neatness, those embellishments of life to high and low, were there in all their freshness and order; and the young couple who flanked the clear fire, with the tea table between them, would have graced any dwelling, however stately. Walter was tall, dark, at the first view, grave-looking—but the light that lay in the clear depths of his hazel eyes, the waving hair that fell off in sable masses from his broad, white forehead, and the pleasant curve of the mouth, all aided the expression that played like light and shade on a mountain side, over his somewhat strongly marked features, and sombre, black brows. Sense, determination, and good humour, were blended in that face, and a world of love flashed in his glances, as he looked at the blue-eyed, auburn-tressed, blocming little fairy, who was pouring out his tea, and who, from the crown of her graceful head, to the sole of her saucy bit of a foot, was so dainty, delicate, arch, and provoking, that she amply justified the tender and triumphant glance her husband bent upon her. And yet, as the meal went on, Jessy was conscious of a something—perhaps the prescience of her love had divined it before his coming—a something that troubled her husband that night more than usual. She saw it lingering behind the flashes of his loving glance; she heard it in the tones of his voice, like a sigh struggling to break in upon its music; and when the tea things were removed and the fire stirred for a rousing blaze, Jessy sat herself on a hassock that brought her head close to her husband's knee, and taking one of his long, brown hands in both hers, without looking up, said—

"What is it, Walter—any new disaster—tell me dear?"

"Oh, nothing new," replied Walter, coughing down a sigh, nervously. Then after a pause, through his shut teeth he added, half abstractedly, "It's tough work, Jessy, my girl! rowing against wind and tide—tough work. But I am not going to give in though." He released his hand from Jessy's clasp, and smote it down on the table with a thump, and then, as if apologetically, he laid it tenderly on her head. The blue eyes looked brightly up from under the shadow of the pent-house hand, and Jessy said—

"Give in, indeed! Never. Faint heart never won fair lady."

"Ah, my Jessy, that's true; but Fortune is more fickle than fair, and often an unprincipled jade to boot. She's harder to win, honestly, than a certain fair lady I know of."

"Hush! heretic, rebel, mutineer—what shall I call you? It's not true;" yet, she added after a little pause, "you know every one says a medical man cannot get a practice in a day."

"No, Jessy; but we have been here two years, and we are farther off than at first."

"Oh, Walter; and the poor people are always coming to you, and—"

"And the rich, Jessy? they desert me; and I would bide my time, little wife, but you make a coward of me."

"I! Why, Walter—now, that's not fair. I may make a brave man braver—a strong man stronger—but a coward! No, that I shall never make you. If being true, and honest, and faithful to principle is not the way to success, why it's not we that are ruined, it's the world."

"Well, Jessy, and if so, it amounts to the same thing."

"No, Walter. People who have health and youth, and honesty and talent, are not, and cannot be ruined. That's the best capital, I've heard you say twenty times; and depend on it, Walter, that Mr. Treboosy will be found out; for although people take drink freely themselves, they do not like a drinking doctor."

"They like his prescriptions, my Jessy! and this very day I have lost my election as parish surgeon. Mr. Accrid, the distiller, and Gullem, the vintner, were at the board, and the guardians decided on re-instating Treboosy."

A flush was on Jessy's cheek, and a tear in her eye, for she knew that the appointment of parish surgeon, though involving great labour and poor pay, was of the utmost importance to her husband, as it brought his professional skill into repute and aided him in getting a practice—so that by these tidings even her buoyant spirits were checked, and, still caressing her husband's hand, she was silent, wondering, meanwhile, that people should trust their own lives, and mourning that the poor who could not help themselves

should be trusted, to the care of a man noted for intemperance, and of whose neglect and cruelty to his pauper patients
she had heard soul-harrowing details. Ah! Jessy had yet
to learn that the world is very lenient to those whose vices
are popular, so long as those vices only injure the poor; and
she had equally to learn that virtue, if it condemns the
practice of the majority, is sure to engender malice. Her
husband's determination to live soberly, and to give sober
remedies to his patients, was the hinderance to his success.
He neither would drink with them, nor sanction their drinking. People who wanted the flimsy pretext of medical prescription to quiet their consciences—ladies who desired to
quote their doctor as advising port or sherry, bottled porter,
or a dash of spirits now and then, were annoyed at the young
surgeon, and soon returned to that kind, good soul, Treboosy
—who, poor fellow, was no cne's enemy but his own.

The reverie of the young couple was disturbed by the
sound of a horse's gallop, that, in the lull of the wind,
seemed to be approaching near. "Called out on such a
night, Walter," was the sentence hardly out of Jessy's lips,
when they heard a well-known voice shouting, "Here, Jack,
take my horse. Is Mr. Elton within?"

"Why it's uncle Smithson, Jessy, come to see us at last,
and on such a night as this," Without a moment's delay
both husband and wife hastened into the passage, and met
their unexpected visitor on the threshold with many words
of greeting, mingled with a surprise they could not check.

In a little time, the visitor was divested of all his wraps,
and seated cozily in the snug seat Walter had just vacated,
with his feet resting on the hassock that had served for
Jessy's perch, and while he refreshed himself with tea, the
young couple learned that their relative, who was a physician, had been called in to a consultation at a neighbouring
town, and preferred taking a bed at his nephew's to riding
fifteen miles across the moor to his own house on such a
night.

Walter Elton was almost as much surprised to hear that
his uncle had been at a consultation, as he had been to see
him in his house that night. For Dr. Smithson had suddenly given up practice some years before, no one knew

why, though, as he wrote extensively on medical subjects, it became gradually the general opinion that he wanted to devote himself to the literature of his profession. His skill was undoubted, but he refused all applications, though his means were far from ample. He it was who had brought up his orphan nephew, Walter Elton, and had implanted the strict temperance principle which the young surgeon so fully carried out; as yet, it must be owned, to his professional injury. At the urgent solicitation of an old personal friend, Dr. Smithson had attended this evening's consultation, and was now making brief but keen inquiries about his young relative's prospects, and hearing the reluctantly expressed fears as to ultimate success which Walter, in his replies, could not suppress.

Dr. Smithson was a small, thin man, with an anxious nervous expression of countenance. He was bald, his high forehead was furrowed with deep lines of care rather than age, and an agitated twitching of the mouth told a tale of irresolution that the clear, grey eyes contradicted. There was evidently a contest in his nature. His reason clear, prompting him to firmness; his feelings acute, betraying him to weakness. He heard his nephew's discouraging statement with an agitated look, and then fell into a deep reverie, which neither Jessy nor Walter disturbed by a single word. At length, rousing himself, he looked from one to the other, and said, " You find keeping a conscience expensive, no doubt; but you must not flag, for, if you do not cling to conscience as a friend, it will cling to you as an enemy." A sigh, so heavy that little Jessy looked scared, followed the words, and the speaker after a while resumed, saying, " I'll open a page of my experience for you—a page I had thought closed for ever,—and, if you are halting, irresolute as to your course, what I have to tell may be useful. You know, Walter, that I was in practice at Mill-Regis for many years; but you do not know why I gave up my prospects of a successful career in an honourable profession, and sunk in the prime of my life into a mere recluse. Well, you shall hear. Among my patients was the family of a merchant, one of those delightful households that remind one of a better world. Mr. and Mrs. Morrell, Miss Digby, Mrs.

D

Morrell's sister, and a lovely group of well-trained children, comprised the family. If ever there was a perfectly happy home in this world, it was theirs. The father, though a keen business man, was God-fearing, and full of tender and wise consideration in his family. Mrs. Morrell and her sister were not only very cultivated, but very gifted women. It had been an early marriage of the heads of the household— Mrs. Morrell was not more than thirty when her seventh child was born, her husband was some four years older, her sister five years younger. I became the friend as well as physician of this family. I may add, though that concerns no one but myself, that I had hopes—Maria Digby inspired them—of being their relative." Uncle Smithson paused a moment here, to swallow down a sigh, and continued—" You must not think these women lived for themselves and their own homestead only. They were the friends of the poor in the best sense—they helped them to help themselves. In the schools, by the bed of sickness and death, amid the daily struggles of decent industry, there were Mrs. Morrell and Maria, instructing, comforting, aiding. And, though gratitude is very rare, yet I am bound to say, that the names of my friends were rarely uttered without a blessing. It was considered a public calamity in the town of Mill-Regis when Mrs. Morrell met with an accident that injured the knee joint, and threatened serious consequences. You know the fame of C——, the celebrated surgeon ; he was my coadjutor in the treatment of the case. Though he was consulted at a very early stage, his skill was baffled, and there was no hope of saving the limb. When amputation was resolved on, I trembled for the result, for Mrs. Morrell's constitution had been weakened by the many demands her numerous family had made on it. Though but a young woman, she had not the elasticity of youth, and we resorted, both before and after the operation, to stimulants, to sustain nature, as we said. She bore the amputation with the fortitude women pre-eminently show in operations, but I confess I had my doubts about the regimen prescribed for my patient. I had misgivings that the nature of these stimulants, so freely ordered by the faculty, had never been sufficiently studied. They are a convenient and popular prescription, but I was conscious that a fit of illness, or a pro-longed attendance on the sick, often brought on the worst of all maladies—intemperance. I knew that women were often the victims of medical advice, but coward that I was, I yielded my judgment, stifled my convictions. The luxurious, delicious, deceptive potion was taken daily in all innocence, by Mrs. Morrell, and soon looked for with eagerness; relished, relied on, found indispensable. For two months she lay in imminent peril; then in a fitful way she began to mend. She was fearfully harassed with neuralgic pains. Narcotics as well as stimulants were freely administered. She bore her sufferings with patient sweetness, and her fine mind long surmounted the horrors both of her malady and her medicines. Oh! to think of her clinging to life for her children's sake—willing to suffer and to try all things if she might be restored, mutilated cripple as she was, to train the little group, whose pictures hung round her room to feast her eyes when she was for weeks too weak to have them brought to her. And yet, though the mother's heart-strings were pulled earthward by little hands, there were times when the soul soared heavenward, and with an unfaltering tongue she could say, 'Not my will, but Thine be done.'

"Her sister's love and care were so constant that her health began to suffer. I had placed an experienced nurse with Mrs. Morrell from the commencement of her illness; and as the more urgent symptoms abated, Miss Digby gave her attention more fully to the three children who were at home—the four eldest had been placed at school. Things were in this state when calling, as was my custom the last thing at night, I was startled by a strange incoherence in Mrs. Morrell's manner. She had been weeping bitterly, and appeared all at once to feel how helpless she had become, and must ever remain. No person in health can, perhaps, estimate the anguish with which a young and beautiful woman, beloved and admired, finds herself suddenly an object of pity, maimed, and dependent for life. I tried to comfort her, but she resented my condolence; and I left her with the thought that her fine temper and spirit were both worn by her trials, and that it would be advisable to remove her as soon as possible to a cottage Mr. Morrell had taken on

the banks of Mill-Regis river, three miles south of the town.
In about three weeks from the evening in question, on a
splendid July day, the invalid was removed to her pleasant
retreat, where the river flowed peacefully before the cottage,
and deep woods in the rear extended for miles. I was satisfied with the immediate effects of this change, though I
never saw again the look of resignation that had been so
affecting in the early stages of her illness. She became
abstracted, melancholy, querulous; and I was startled by
Maria asking me one day whether such continued potions of
strong drink, as the nurse administered, could be either
necessary or safe? I found, on inquiry, that my original
prescription had been doubled in quantity. In vain I tried
to reduce the dose. Sleeplessness and terrible neuralgia
wore the sufferer, or deep despondency threatened to settle
down upon her. I would have given my right arm to have
undone the injury that stimulants, scientifically prescribed,
were doing to both mind and body. I called in a medical
friend, experienced in disease of the brain, and he treated
my fears lightly, and, above all things, protested against any
reduction of either narcotics or stimulants. Uneasy, and
apprehending I knew not what, I redoubled my attention,
and as summer waned into autumn, I became convinced that
the nurse was not a safe person to administer stimulants,
either as medicine or beverage. We talk with horror of
poisonings—these professional nurses have one poison ever
at hand that kills more than all the rest put together.

"I communicated my dissatisfaction to Mr. Morrell, who
was at the time at his counting-house at Mill-Regis. He
went immediately to the cottage, deliberating how to effect
the removal of the nurse without agitating his wife. To his
great relief Mrs. Morrell made a complaint that the nurse
talked to her in the night and prevented her sleeping, and
proposed that the woman's bed should be removed to the
adjoining room. As this seemed to meet the difficulty half
way, and to be a preliminary that would lead soon to the
dismissal of the nurse, my friend assented to the plan, and
left his wife's sofa considerably relieved. He then looked in
upon his children who were with Miss Digby in the nursery.
Pressing business compelled him to return and pass the

night at Mill-Regis, and when he parted from his wife he remembered afterwards that she called him back and said—'Edward, dear! forgive me all the trouble I have caused you.'

"'Forgive,' that's a wrong word, he answered, and so is 'trouble.'

"'Never mind, Edward,' she insisted, 'let me say the words once more, Forgive me, dear!'

"He humoured her request, for the tears were brimming her eyes—and they parted. Ah! never to meet again.

"Mrs. Morrell's apartments were two parlours on the left hand side of the little entrance hall. They were convenient, as she could be carried from her bed to the sofa in the sitting room more easily than up and down a staircase; and it was settled that the nurse, that night, should remove her chair bed into the front parlour, and Mrs. Morrell, alluding to herself, expressed a hope that 'she would have rest and quiet.' She insisted on the folding doors between the rooms being closed, and a table put against them, and when the nurse urged that she must come to give the patient medicine in the night, Mrs. Morrell said—'Come at five o'clock, I will not take it earlier.'

"Maria, as was her wont, read and prayed at her sister's bedside; thought her unusually composed, and without any misgiving, left her for the night, merely telling the nurse aside, to go into her room about one o'clock, but not to speak to the invalid unless the latter spoke.

"It was a rainy night, and the back windows were beaten with heavy showers. Once Maria woke, and thought she heard a cracking sound. She slipped out on the landing, looked over the stairs, and saw the nurse returning from the bed-room, along the passage, to the front parlour. Miss Digby did not speak, but looking at her watch by the twilight, she saw it was one o'clock. Pleased with this proof of the nurse's vigilance, she retired to rest, and slept soundly for three hours, when she was awoke by a loud shriek. She sat up—the cry was repeated; her name was called frantically by the nurse. To leap out of bed, throw a dressing-gown round her, and rush down stairs, was the work of a moment. All was darkness. The nurse had risen to visit her patient, and on entering the room was startled, to find her night light extinguished. Returning to fetch her own candle, as tremblingly she re-entered the chamber, a strong gust of wind blew it out. She called to her mistress and rushing forward past the foot of the bed, the drifting rain dashed upon her face from the open window. Her screams of horror and her wild call had brought Maria to the room, who instantly laid her hands upon the bed—it was empty!

" 'What have you done with my sister?' was the momentary cry; for, as she afterwards explained, the helplessness of the invalid was so complete—she had never yet been able to use a crutch, and was lifted about like an infant—that the idea of her moving of herself never entered her mind. Fearing she knew not what, Maria went back to her room, procured a light, and returned to the bewildered nurse, still demanding, 'Where is my sister—what have you done with her?'

" She was not in the room, and, looking from the window, the fitful moonlight struggling through a wild wrack of clouds, showed them nothing but the wet garden path, and the dripping boughs of trees swept by the wild, autumn gale. To leap down from the window, and run along the path, followed by the shrieking nurse, was Maria's first impulse. No voice replied to their calls, and a terrible instinct led her to a well at the very bottom of the long garden. Even in the darkness of the morning, she found that the cover of the well, placed there as a precaution against accident to the children, had been removed, and by the brink Maria's feet were entangled in some obstacle. She lifted it in her hands, and by the feel she knew it was Mrs. Morrell's Angola shawl! The maid servants, aroused by the cries, after what seemed to the distracted sister a dreadful delay, brought lanterns to the well, and there in its depths, to their amazement as well as horror, lay, in the stillness of death, the well-known form. It was a shock that might well madden the brain of the beholder; and a panic seized Maria, so that, involuntarily wrapping the wet shawl she had found over her dressing-gown, she fled, with bare feet and head, through the woods that intervened between the cottage and Mill-Regis, and never stopped till she fell senseless at her brother's door. A policeman who saw her fall, and recognised her, roused the household. In a few minutes, the tidings of some terrible catastrophe spread. Mr. Morrell, followed by many friends I among the number, hastened to the cottage. Meanwhile help had been procured, and two labouring men had succeeded in bringing up the corpse. When I entered the house, and passed through to the garden, not knowing what to expect, the cold glimmer of early dawn showed me a ghastly sight—Mrs. Morrell, her drenched clothes so tightly fastened and bound round her, that all doubt as to her dying by her own hands was removed, lay on the little lawn—her children's play place! The husband, pale as a spectre, was kneeling on the wet grass, embracing the marble looking form, and mingling cries of agony with terms of endearment. A voice within me, as I approached that prostrate form—that frenzied husband—said, 'This is your work.' Ah, Walter and Jessy, you may start and say, 'No.' I tell you both what my soul tells me, strong drink disorganised the fine fabric of that brain, and laid it in ruins. And I—fool that I was! —I ordered that strong drink. She might have rallied well; or at all events, she might have died a death her family could have remembered without horror—a death in which God's hand was seen and reverenced, but for that accursed remedy. Remedy! forsooth. The science that upholds such a remedy may well be called the 'destructive art of healing.'"

Heavy drops of perspiration rolled down Dr. Smithson's face as he spoke, and a painful silence followed, which Walter broke, by saying, abstractedly, "It is the most singular suicide I ever heard of, in the weak state you describe."*

"Yes; it was a preternatural effort, the result of stimulants. She had dropped from the window, and crawled three hundred yards down the garden path to the well, and, more strangely still, had lifted the heavy cover, which was a man's work;—poor thing! her hands were bruised with the effort, and her clothes torn and dabbled, though the care with which she had secured her attire showed that instincts of modesty and neatness had survived her reason."

"What became of the family?"

---

* This case is a literal fact. The scene only, for obvious reasons, is altered.

"Ah, don't ask me," replied Dr. Smithson, with a groan, "that was not the only death. Maria, the good, true-hearted sister, never recovered the shock; what, with the fright, and the exposure to the weather, a rheumatic fever came on. No serious apprehensions were entertained, but the disease attacked the heart, and in five weeks after, all that was mortal of that gentle creature shared the grave of her poor sister. Morrell disposed of his business, and took his motherless children to America, where I hear he lives a secluded life, stricken beyond the help of man. For me, too, that night was a crisis. Tortured by remorse, haunted by the pale face of the victim, and the upbraiding eyes of Maria, who had always remonstrated against the use of stimulants, my nerves were shaken, my confidence gone; I gave up my practice, and went abroad, as you remember."

"But no one ever blamed you, Uncle."

"No; but my own conscience blamed me. For a time I was a wanderer. I visited the most famous hospitals in Europe, and gave myself up to study. I rallied, and wrote as you know—not, I trust, without benefit to science; but the practical part of the noble art for which I was trained has been to me a dead letter from that time. Perhaps, in this I have been wrong. I do not set myself up to you, Walter, as an example—nay, I am a warning. Let me charge you never to pander to the diseased appetite, or the common prejudice, by recklessly prescribing these dangerous and insidious drinks. The moral effects of medicines, the formation of bad habits, ought not to be lost sight of by the medical philosopher. He should be the friend of his patients. Oh! Walter, I was the enemy of mine, and where I most wanted to be as a friend and brother."

"Dear Sir," interposed Jessy, as she ventured to take the hand that Dr. Smithson had pressed to his brow, and clasp it in hers, "we were talking when you came in of Walter's determination to abide by temperance principles in his treatment of patients, and though we were a little low-spirited at the difficulties, the tastes, and customs of society at present, your warning of to-night will confirm Walter, I am sure,"

"It ought," said Walter, "unless I mean to degenerate into one of those mercenary wretches, who gloat on a patient's sufferings for the sake of his gold. My enemy, Treboosy, may act as he pleases. I'll pursue the sober course."

"Treboosy; what of him?" said Dr. Smithson.

"Oh, only the board of guardians to-day said, I was crotchety with my temperance, and elected him their medical officer."

"Well, if they did, he'll not be able to accept the post. The police are by this time after him. His career has been long and reckless, but it's over. I was called in by my old friend, Farmer Sutton, of the Grange, who begged me to see his housekeeper, and met Dr. Quicksett. The poor woman was dying, and from poison. Treboosy, from his own surgery, sent her a lotion, and labelled it as a dose in his own handwriting. He had been dining with some choice spirits, at the Fountain———, a fiery fountain, slipped home for a few minutes, to see about some prescriptions; his young man was out, and the muddle-headed fellow made this fatal blunder. This is the third awkward case in Treboosy's practice in a few months. The others were neglect, and he managed to get over them, but this is palpable. I'm amazed, not only at the want of caution, but of compunction in these tipplers; but public indignation is aroused, and all the distillers and vintners in the district will not be able to screen a wretch who has long had the curses of the poor on his murderous practice. So, if Treboosy has been your obstacle, Walter, that's removed. But I warn you by the failure of others, whatever be the cost, 'keep a conscience.'"

The young surgeon made the promise, not merely to his uncle, but to his own soul in the sight of God; and though old topers talked of his whims, and young tipplers would have liked to drink genteelly by medical advice, and therefore were for a time cool to him, his skill, promptitude, and real kindness, gradually won him the patronage of the rich, in addition to that which he had long had—the blessing of the poor.

FACT—NOT FICTION.

"Why did she love him ? Fool, be still ;
Is human love the growth of human will ?"

BYRON.

"IF you know anything very remarkably out of the common way, do not relate it, or your reputation for veracity may suffer," is the sentiment in substance, if not in words, of Lord Chesterfield ; and perhaps very cautious people, who think more of their own reputation than the interests of society, might act on such a maxim. But truth, whether it approaches the marvellous, and thus transcends ordinary experience, or merely presents every-day realities, is ever its own justification, and therefore the following strange but strictly true narrative is presented to the reader with only an alteration of names.

Twelve years ago this winter, I passed a week at a pretty sea-side town on the south coast of England. As this place rose chiefly during the administration of the " Heaven-born Minister," (?) I will call it Pittville. The landlady of the house where I lodged interested me greatly. She was about twenty-five or twenty-six, and very lovely. I was struck with her blooming complexion, luxuriant light-brown hair, small features, and clear, earnest, grey eyes—shaded, in strong contrast to her fairness, by long, black eyelashes—while the small but well-proportioned form, light, firm carriage, gave one an idea, not only of beauty, but of character ; which first impression was amply confirmed by a clear voice and a most sweet, intelligent manner of speaking. I had been two days in the house when I caught a glimpse of the husband of this fair creature. He was more than twice her age, cross and sickly looking, and very lame. I saw him from my parlour window coming up the little front garden, leaning on his crutch, and should not have given more than a casual glance at him, but I noticed my hostess, whom I will call Mrs. Questo, run down the walk, meet the cripple half-way, and taking the arm that was not engaged with the crutch, draw it within her own, and look smilingly into the sallow face that repaid her with a testy, impatient glance. It was a curious picture—she so young, bright, and healthy—he so worn, dark, and feeble. "Can that poor creature be her father?" was my mental query as I saw her look of tenderness, and the care with which she helped the feeble steps of the lame. It jarred sadly on my feelings to hear, just after a harsh voice in the passage saying, "You're mighty officious! I can do very well without you're jigging out into the cold. I wish to goodness you'd let me alone."

A short time after, Mrs. Questo entered my room, and I saw her eyes were red with weeping, and she apologised for some omission by saying, " My husband is not well to-day, and it makes me anxious. I felt him tremble as I helped him up the walk."

I was silent from astonishment. Her husband! That cross-grained cripple! Somehow, during that day my hostess sunk in my estimation. "Such a choice! Oh, she is only a pretty simpleton; and I thought her so intelligent," was my thought. Shakspere's words rose in my memory :—

> " It is a judgment maimed, and most imperfect,
> That will confess perfection so could err
> Against all rules of nature."

Yet these words applied to Desdemona—one of the purest and sweetest of Shakspere's female characters.

The evening before I was to leave, Mrs. Questo said she wanted to speak to me. As I requested her to take the chair opposite me, and the grey twilight of the winter's afternoon was deepening into night, I broke up the fire into a cheerful blaze, and sat watching the face of my hostess, as her features were now touched with light, now softened in shadow, by the fitful gleam of the dancing flame. Gradually, as she spoke, my attention was wholly given to her words, which, as nearly as possible, were to this effect :—

"As you travel a great deal, and know many places, I thought I would ask you if you know any one of the name of Gellerie, or Getterie—Mrs. General Gellerie—I want to find a lady of that name." I answered in the negative, and added, "General! all widows or wives of generals are easily enough found; an Army List or Court Guide can give you that information."

"Ah, this lady is a foreigner; we have advertised in the *Times*, and in *Galignani*, over and over again, and had some answers, but none from or of the person we seek. And we are told to give the matter up; but *I* cannot give it up—oh, never!"

"Why are you so anxious?" I said. "Oh, it's a sad story," she replied. "Our friends know it well. I've told it often, but never without anguish. I feel I must tell you. I am one of a large family. My father was a pilot, my mother—poor dear soul!—is one of the best of mothers. The three eldest of their children were sons, then seven daughters, and last, six years after me—I'm the youngest girl—another son— George! my little brother, George." She paused—coughed away a sob in her throat, and resumed. "My father for years was one of the steadiest and best pilots on this coast. He earned, as he ought, a good income in his dangerous calling; and we had a comfortable home, in a plain way. My mother brought her children up well. She was a Christian woman, knew her duty, and did it tenderly and faithfully. Yes! I've heard that for years they had as happy a home as any in Pittville, but *I* do not remember much comfort. My eldest brother, a youth of sixteen when I was born, went out with my father in his boat. A captain of a vessel had given father a keg of brandy. It was a cold night; and the habit of drinking had been for some time creeping slowly upon my poor father; he took a great deal of brandy himself, and, thinking to keep out the cold, he gave my brother James far more than the lad had ever taken in his life. A sudden squall came on, and the boat, owing to neglecting the sail, capsized. My brother was drowned, and my father was rescued from a watery grave by my husband, who was then a strong, young man. But in the struggle of that night poor Questo strained his leg. The case was somewhat mismanaged, and shrinking of the limb, and confirmed lameness was the consequence. My father never recovered the effects of that night. He was conscious that he was not sober when the accident happened, and he could not bear his remorse of conscience about my brother's death. From that time, though he never was seen drunk, or known to be a drunkard, he drank very hard. The most dangerous of all drinkers, I think, are those who, as they say, carry drink well.

"What I remember of home in my childhood was—my mother's face, worn with grief; my elder brothers glad to get away from it; my sisters working hard at needlework, and seldom, with all our toil, gaining the means to keep out want; my father's presence like a cloud that spread darkness over our dwelling, his absence a constant anxiety—no peace for my poor mother any way. This was the state of things, when another baby came. Our family were rather spoken of for being good looking (a hesitation was in the narrator's tone as she thus modestly alluded to personal gifts), but this infant was noticed by every one for his extreme beauty. My parents loved him, not only as their youngest child, but for his wonderful resemblance to the son who had found an untimely death, though I think we are all much alike, except myself, I'm the smallest and plainest of the family.

"My father very imprudently became bond for a man, who absconded, and left him to pay the debt, which swept away all that the care of my mother had kept together, in the ebbing tide of our fortunes as a family. My two next elder sisters and myself would have had no schooling, if William Questo, after his long illness, had not come to lodge in our house, and spent his evenings in teaching us. My husband is now a schoolmaster, but his bad health is sadly against him. He goes out, you may have noticed, daily to the school-room, only five minutes' walk, yet you see how exhausted he comes home. Well, as I was saying, we came to poverty—bitter poverty! Often there was hardly bread for us, hard as my mother and sisters worked. When I was eight years old, and my brother George two, a lady came down from London and took lodgings near our house. We had a cottage by the sea; that has long been pulled down to make room for the Royal Crescent. When I used to be nursing

and playing with George in the garden, the lady would look
over our gate and speak to us.   Then she came with little
gifts of fruit and toys, and so won our love, that we were
always on the look out for our kind friend.   She taught the
child to call her 'mamma,'—and, as she was in deep
mourning, the story went that Mrs. Smith was a widow, and
and had lost her only child.

"Somehow, my mother never liked to hear little George
call her 'mamma,' and would try to make the child substi-
tute the name of 'lady;' but George, with infantile wilful-
ness, would always add mamma, so that it became a pet
name with him to greet Mrs. Smith as 'lady mamma.'   As
the place began to fill with autumn visitors, Mrs. Smith said
she must go to see an aunt at Calais, and asked my mother
to let me and my brother go with her.   She would be back
in a month.   My mother refused; she could not part with
her boy, for she seemed to know he was the lady's pet, and
I was to be but her attendant.   My father was indignant at
my mother's refusal.   He said she was injuring her child,
and preventing his having, perhaps, a fortune given him.   In
his drink of an evening he would fill the house with misery
by his scolding, and this continued till he wore out my
mother's spirits, and she gave her consent reluctantly to our
paying this visit.

"My little brother was carried by my father on board the
packet, and as Mrs. Smith took the child from him in the
ladies' cabin, where she immediately repaired, I saw her put
a bit of paper into his hands.   'God bless you, madam,' faltered my father.   'I'll be on the look-out on the 3d of Oc-
tober for your return, and you'll please write a line as soon
as you get across; for my wife, poor soul, can't bear the boy
out of her sight; and it's hard for me, madam—but little
Liddy—my name is Lydia—will help you to take care of
him.'   I remember he passed the back of his hand across
his eyes for a moment, then thrust the bit of paper, with a
sigh, into his pocket, kissed me twice, and, without looking
again at the child, rushed up the cabin stairs.   We were soon
under weigh; and I would have liked to have gone on deck,
but Mrs. Smith insisted on my lying down by her side, and as
George soon fell asleep, we were all lying on a broad sofa

covered up with her mantle, and never showed our faces until, in less than three hours, we were at Calais. An old French lady met us at the pier, and embraced Mrs. Smith and my brother most rapturously—when the little fellow, half frightened at the old lady, cried out 'Mamma! lady mamma!' and hid his face in Mrs. Smith's bosom, the old lady both laughed and wept with delight.

"We went to an hotel in the Grand Place of Calais, and soon after taking some refreshments, I put my brother to bed in Mrs. Smith's bed, and occupied a little crib in a recess of the same room. The next day Mrs. Smith said we were to go into the country to see a féte, called, in that part of France, a Ducâss. We went accordingly to some woods about seven miles off, where, on the green sward round a monument erected to commemorate the falling of the first balloon, and amid the pleasant glades of a wood, there were dancing and festivity that I and little George enjoyed greatly. It was a warm September day, and I was thirsty. It was not water or milk they gave me, but wine, probably not very strong, but still stronger than I was used to, and all I recollect is like a dream, of people dancing among green trees, until waking up, as it seems to me, I found myself in a little bed in a strange place. I sat up, everything swam round with me, I was deadly sick, and my cries brought a woman to the side of the shelf-like bed. I was on board a steamer! and the stewardess, a Frenchwoman, spoke such poor English, I could understand nothing. After a time the sickness passed off, the lamp was extinguished, I was helped out of bed, dressed, and told to go on deck. Up I went in the bright morning sunlight, and began to seek for Mrs. Smith and my brother. I could not find them. The vessel was not on the sea, but on a river. Custom-house officers put off from a little town in a boat, and came on board, and I heard a lady say 'Thank God, we are in the Thames, in two or three hours we shall be in London.' I ran down to the stewardess, and now in a great panic, asked for my brother. 'Oh! the lady say she will follow, come after you soon: and see! you are all right, your route is put all down on dis card,' and she pointed to a ticket I had not seen, hung round my neck, with directions to my home, and my little travelling bag had a similar ticket. One of the passengers, a French gentleman, was to take me to the train for the south coast. I had all sorts of childish thoughts about her having been too late, and missed the vessel, and so, at about nine o'clock, I took my French conductor's hand, landed at the London docks, had some breakfast with him, and in two hours was on my road home. There was no one to meet me, and I carried my carpet bag myself. When I entered my mother's door and stood before her, I was received with a shriek of wonder and terror. 'George! my boy! where is he?' I could only tell what I have told you, adding, what I believed, that Mrs. Smith would come. 'She will never come!' raved my poor mother, 'it is a trick, I see it all; she has stolen my child!' And so it proved; from that day to this we have heard no tidings either of my brother or the cruel woman who kidnapped him! The French gentleman who had put me into the train was found, the stewardess also was examined, and their testimony was that an English lady put me on board the vessel saying, I was her nurse-girl in England, and she wanted to send me home. I was half asleep when brought on board, and was immediately put to bed, the stewardess promising to take care of me, and the French gentleman agreeing to see me to the train, as he was going to the station. There all clue was lost, except that my elder sisters remembered seeing the envelope of a letter directed to Mrs. General Gellerie; whether it was two l's or two uncrossed t's in the middle of the name, they could not say; and on inquiry at the post-office, we found that Mrs. Smith called for letters that the postmaster remembered were so directed, but no passport in that name had been taken.

"Heavy as the blow was to my mother, it was heavier to my father. He never smiled or looked up after. 'I sold my child. Yes! the wretch gave me five pounds when I put the darling into her arms, and I drank it, beast that I was— worse than beast, monster, devil!' These were my father's words. Morning, noon, and night, he never rested. Mistaken friends gave him drink to cheer him up. It set his brain on fire. He died at last, raving mad.

"These troubles completed our ruin. My mother would not have had a roof to shelter her but for him who is now

my husband. He paid the rent, taught us younger girls—
and that so well, that three of my sisters are certificated
schoolmistresses, doing well, and the three elder are
married."

"And you also!" I said, as my narrator paused. "Yes!
it was all he asked, after his years of kindness. My mother
was going to live with my eldest married sister,—that was
nine years after we lost dear George, and I was then nine-
teen. He, my husband, you see, had, as it were, brought
me up. He could not be left alone, desolate, after all he had
done ; and so—and so, you see, we were married." Either
she blushed, or the glow of the fire was on her face. Perhaps, at that instant, she did not like the expression on my
countenance, for she lifted her head proudly, looked steadily
into my eyes and said, "Yes, we married ; and I am thank-
ful for a good man's love."

"Bravo," said I, mentally; "true wife! This crusty
tempered cripple of yours may have—nay, certainly has—a
soul fairer and larger than is given to half the straight-legged,
curled darlings of the world."

Five years after the time this incident was told me, I
went again to Pittville, and without any previous announcement, I drove at once to my old lodgings. Mrs. Questo, now
a woman of thirty-three, looking brighter and happier than
I had ever seen her, rushed into the passage as she heard my
voice, and welcomed me with a sort of jubilant caress.

"Oh, come in! You will be our guest now. We don't
take lodgers," were the words rapidly and laughingly uttered.

"Why, how gay you are," I said. "Gay!" she replied,
"to be sure I am ; we have found my brother!" at these
words, in the most absurd way we ran into each others em-
brace, and began kissing and crying.

"Found ; oh do tell me all about it," said I, as soon as I
could command voice ; and throwing myself, all cloaked and
bonnetted, into an arm-chair.

"Take off your things first." "No! no! I don't stir till
you tell me. Quick, quick ; how did you find him?"
"Well, we had a barrister, Mr. Fitzedwin, came last spring
to take lodgings with us ; he brought his wife with him, but
my husband did not like them as lodgers ; he suspected that

E

the lady was not in reality the wife of Mr. Fitzedwin; and before they had been here a week he gave them notice to quit. I wanted to ask him, as I did every one, whether he knew the name of " Gellerie," but owing to the anger he showed at receiving notice to go, I could not summon up courage; and the lady was very haughty; but on the morning that they were leaving, Mr. Fitzedwin called from the passage up the stairs to his wife, to tell her a letter he expected had come, and mentioned the name—the same—yet how different! that had so long been lingering imperfectly in the recesses of my memory. I knew it at once. The old lady in France had been called it. His words were, 'Gengouilliére has agreed to take my old office.' I was in the parlour. I rushed instantly into the passage, and taking his arm in my eagerness, I said, 'Do, pray sir, say that name again! do tell me who it is you know of that name?'

" He laughed good-temperedly at me, and replied, 'Know Gengouilliére? I should think I did. Why? Do you want him?' 'I have long wished to find a lady, and also a gentleman of that name,' I answered, as his lady came down stairs. 'Well! here's his address,' he said, tearing off the top of the note, and giving it to me. In a moment more they were gone, and I was so intent on the direction, that I forgot to thank him. 'No. — Blank Court, Lombard Street.' I could not wait for my husband's return, I ran to the school and showed him the direction, and pronounced the name, he laughed at me, I mean he scolded me rather, but that's his way when he's pleased, and would not consent to my going up at once to London, nor let me write to my mother who was in London with my eldest sister, but, as I left him, I heard him say, 'Can we have all been so foolish as to take the prefix " Gen " of the name for an abbreviated title?' and by that shewed he thought we were on the right track.

" At night he consented to my going up by express train the next morning and finding 'Blank Court.' I never slept that night. I was in London at eleven o'clock, and in a quarter of an hour, I stood in a paved court, reading the names painted on the sides of a doorway that led to many offices. Among them was Louis Emmanuel Gengouillière, Stock and Share Broker. I went up a flight of stairs to the office indicated, and going in, saw some clerks sitting at a desk that extended across the room. My heart beat so that my voice was nearly inaudible, but I managed to make them understand I wanted to see Mr. Gengouillière. ' He is not here to-day,' said a young man. A youth near him said in an audible whisper, ' It's the Derby-day—I fancy he's off to Epsom.' 'No!' replied the first speaker, 'his aunt is very ill.'

" ' Does he not live here ? ' I said.

" ' Here! This is his office ; his private residence is near Tottenham.' He gave me a card with the address, and I left. Fortunately the Tottenham omnibuses, as I knew, went constantly from Bishopsgate Street, and without more than a few minutes' delay, I was on the road. I had shown the card to the conductor, who seemed to know it. He put me down at the gate of a large mansion, with a carriage sweep up to the door. I rang at the gate, and then, for the first time, my heart failed me. I must be wrong—it cannot be my brother—what shall I say when they answer the ring ? When the servant, in reply to my inquiry if Mr. Gengouillière was at home, answered ' *Yes !* ' and I faltered out I wanted to speak with him, and was led into a large drawing-room that opened on a lawn at the back of the house, I felt like one in a dream.

" I was relieved by finding the room empty, and being left a few moments to myself. I sat down on a chair that faced the open French window, and commanded a view of the lawn. It was one of the loveliest of early June days, just as spring flushes into summer, and the light green of the trees, so newly dressed in their vernal robes, seemed to laugh in the sunshine, and the smooth lawn spreading under the cloudless sky looked so peaceful. Everything was calm but I. I wished the day had been stormy, the sky cloudy—I could not in my great agitation, bear the calm, unsympathizing face of nature. As these thoughts swept through me, I saw the man servant who had let me in, cross the lawn, as if seeking some one, and enter a little alcove that was almost hidden amid laburnums and lilacs. The servant's search seemed to terminate there. He came back, and a minute or so after a tall, fair gentleman in a loose morning-coat came with a bounding step across the lawn. I turned deadly cold, for at a glance I knew this was my long lost brother. Allowing for the difference of age, he was in all respects the image of my eldest living brother. His quiet word as he entered, 'You have not sent me your name—may I ask your business?' gave me a sort of salutary shock like a cold bath. I rose, stood by the table and held it, to steady my trembling knees.

" 'Sir!' I said, 'do you know a person named Mills?'

" 'Mills—Mills,' he answered, musing; 'I think my aunt told me I was at Nurse in England once with a person of that name, but my mother said she forgot whether that really was the name. I recollect we sought at Scarborough for a person of that name, for I wanted some information a few years ago about my baptismal register.'

" 'Scarborough,' I said—'Mrs. Mills never lived there, but two hundred miles or more south of that.'

" 'Then you know Mrs. Mills—and she was my nurse.'

" 'Oh, sir!' I said, 'how am I to tell you—It's a serious thing—perhaps an unwelcome thing, I have to speak of?'

" 'What do you mean,' he said. 'Compose yourself—what is it you can have to tell me?'

" 'This, Sir!—this—the lady you call your mother had no right to the name. Mrs. Mills, whom you call your nurse—I speak truth—God's solemn truth! she is your mother.'

" At this moment the door of the room opened, and a lady glided in, and seeing us both standing confronting each other, she walked up to him, and linking her arm in his, looked up wonderingly in his face.

" 'Who is the lady, Louis?'

" He, with white lips, rejoined dreamily, 'Say on—say what you have to say.'

" I, terribly confused, replied clumsily, 'What I have to say, further, is for your ear only.'

" 'Why?' gasped the wife, 'what can you—what can any one have to say to my husband that his wife may not hear?' She coloured violently as she spoke, drew her arm from her husband's and stood aloof, looking first at one and then at the other.

" 'Speak!' said he, 'repeat your words, I have no secrets from my wife.'

"I faltered out what I had before said, and added, 'the lady was a cruel monster who stole you.'

"'Do you mean to say,' he replied, 'that I am the child of low people.'

"That speech roused me; all my years of love and sorrow were outraged at the moment.

"'No, Sir!' I said—not '*low* people. You are the son of *poor* people. Your father died mad with grief at losing you. You have two brothers, honest men—they will never trouble you; you have seven sisters—I am one—we want nothing of you; we shall, please God! never disgrace you. I ask you one favour. You have a mother living; a dear, good, infirm, old mother! who has prayed for years to be permitted to have tidings of you before she died. To have found your grave would have been a comfort to her. Let not your pride of station harden your heart to her. Go and see her—it is all I ask.'

"'Why, Louis! the woman may be mad,' said the wife, as her husband sank down on a sofa, and clasping his hands over his eyes, groaned aloud.

"'I am not mad,' I said calmly, for strong emotion now acted like a sedative; 'what I say will bear examination. There is your mother's address,' I added, throwing a card I had prepared upon the table, and turning to leave the room.

"He rose, looked sadly in his wife's face, and said,

"'I have been haunted with the thought ever since mamma—Madame Gengouilliére—died, that there was a mystery, but I never thought of this. Pardon me,' he added, turning to me; 'What you say is so strange, it may well confound me. I cannot receive such a testimony unsupported. Why, I'm an impostor, if what you say is true; but I will think over it.'

"'Do as you please,' I said, pointing to the card, 'only call there.' I left the room and the house. I walked swiftly along the road not feeling the motion of my feet, when the hail of the omnibus conductor, who, less than an hour before, had set me down, and was now returning, recalled me to consciousness. On reaching the city, I took an omnibus to the west end, and was put down at my sister's door. To her I told all, but we feared to agitate my mother just then by stating the whole matter; we only said a person of the name we had long sought was found. The poor soul simply sighed and added, 'How long, O Lord, how long?'

"To our great joy the evening post brought a letter from Tottenham. The writer, my brother, said in it that he would investigate the tidings fully, and would call on us the following morning. On receiving this, my sister and myself resolved to tell my mother all. With our utmost caution, we could not prevent her being fearfully agitated. 'Oh, he never can forgive our selling him so. We forfeited our right to him, and now our claim disgraces him.' She kept saying this, and then with a burst of tears, she would add—'My lost boy! shall I see you once more.' In the morning, I dressed my mother nicely in her best black gown and her widow's cap—her dress since my father's death—and my sister and I both said, as we looked at her tall form and comely face, beautiful even in old age—No man need be ashamed to call her mother.'

"I cannot tell you what we felt, as a double knock came to our door, and the stately form of our long-sought brother entered the little parlour. My mother rose from her chair and lifting her arms, tried to run towards him. She could not move a step. She sank down on her seat fainting. He came towards her, saying, 'Is it, can it be—are you really my mother;' and falling on his knees before her, he rested his head on her lap, and burst into tears. She bent over him; nestled her withered hand in his thick curls, and faintly murmured 'My son—my son.' As soon as we recovered, and had made mother drink a glass of water, a good deal of incoherent talk followed. We told our story, interrupted by answers that involved his story. We talked for full two hours, and in brief we learned this, that Mrs. Smith, or Gengouilliére, had died when George was fourteen years of age. He had always thought himself her son, though she did not always treat him kindly. She indulged very much in stimulants, and under their influence she used to threaten to make a beggar of him, and call him a 'base-born wretch.' At other times she indulged him greatly, but those words dwelt on his mind. He was told his father had died in England when he was but two months old. An

aunt and uncle of his father were living, they had no children, and as his father would have been their heir, though
his marriage in England offended them, he was, in right of
his father, to inherit their property. They made Madame
Gengouilliére an ample allowance, but they only tolerated
her; they loved him. The aunt had told him of his little
nurse-girl Lydia Mills; and how sorry she was that Madame
Gengouilliére would insist on sending her home to England
so quickly. Of course the reason was now obvious. A few
days before Madame Gengouilliére died, she said, 'Louis, I
have a secret to tell you relative to your birth, but I am not
strong enough to-day, I must wait till to-morrow.' On the
morrow she was delirious, and the secret was never told.
The uncle took my brother into his office, initiated him
into commercial life, sent him to England to transact business, and after seeing my brother established for himself, a
member of the Stock Exchange, the old man died, leaving
him the bulk of his property, charged only with a jointure to
his widow, who now, in extreme old age, was residing in my
brother's house. · The most curious thing of the whole was,
that when my brother wanted to be naturalised as an English
subject, he could not find his register either at Scarborough,
where he thought he was born, or at Amiens where he had
been told he was born; and he had a dread that he was the
illegitimate son of M. Gengouilliére, born before the marriage
with the lady he called mother. To prevent any difficulties,
his name, as Louis Emmanuel Gengouilliére, was confirmed
to him, by his uncle, who knew his scruples, going to
the expense of a private bill in the House of Commons, so
that, by Act of Parliament, he had a right to the name he
bore. But here came the trial—'My aunt (as I call her)'
said my brother 'must know.' I was glad to hear him say
that; and to see the frank look that accompanied the words.
That very night, before he slept, he told the aged lady,
saying, 'Leave your money to whom you like, I am no son
of your nephew; but give me still your love, for I was an
innocent impostor.'

"Another odd thing is, that though my brother was soon
convinced—indeed, his lingering suspicion prepared him for
receiving our testimony—though his wife, when she saw my

brother and sister, could not refuse the evidence of her eyes in the likeness, yet the aunt would not believe it. Her rage knew no bounds. She has never seen any of us, and will certainly persist in leaving her property to my brother, out of detestation at what she thinks our conspiracy; and as she has no relations in the world, her obstinacy will injure no one.

"We all met last Christmas. Of course there is so great a difference of education and circumstances between my brothers, that they cannot exactly be companions. But that we were of one family no one could doubt. My brother has settled an annuity on my mother, and that has been a great comfort to us. My husband now, as we have no demands on us from my family, has given up his school, and merely takes private pupils for mathematics.

"'Do your family visit your brother?' I said.

"'*I* do, often,' she replied, 'for he says he belongs to me by right of salvage. I call him 'treasure trove.' He has called his little girl after me—Lydia. I think he has a true brother's heart towards me.'

"'I'm glad of that,' I said. 'If he had not, I should call him any thing but *treasure trove*. If he were a prince he might be proud of you.'"

She smiled and kissed me, and I went up thoughtfully to my room, meeting on the stairs the lame husband.

"You've heard the news?" he said, "the poor fool is happy now."

"Fool!" said I, "that is surely a wrong name."

"No," he said, "all women are fools more or less, and a good thing for us men, it is, that they are so."

A STUMBLE ON THE THRESHOLD.

> "The sacred lowe o' weel placed love
>   Luxuriantly indulge it,
> But never tempt the illicit rove,
>   Though naething should divulge it.
> I waive the quantum o' the sin,
>   The hazard o' concealing,
> But och! it hardens a' within,
>   And petrifies the feeling."
>
> BURNS.

"ONE week, only one short week! Bernard." "One week, one whole, long, tedious, week! Gertrude." This different estimate of a given period was made simultaneously in an under tone, by two young people who were strolling in a pleasant garden on the banks of the Thames, in the lovely twilight of a fine, spring evening. It needed no particular penetration to discover the relative circumstances of the speakers. In the flushed cheek, and downcast eye, and half tremulous steps of the lady; in the triumphant glance, hasty, impatient, tread, and protecting tenderness of her companion, as well as in the low, sighing utterance of each, it was mani-fest they were lovers, with the wedding day drawing near. And though Gertrude spoke with faltering, apprehensive love, Bernard appreciated the affectionate lingering of the heart in the home of her childhood; he knew that

> "Love and life are mysteries,
>   Both blessing and both blest;
> And yet how much they teach the heart,
>   Of trial and unrest."

But for himself, he felt as if he had all to hope and nothing to fear in the future, and his only complaint was that time lagged so wearily, and that he still seemed so far from the completion of his joy. Something of this he expressed in the hush of that deepening twilight, but we are not going to inflict upon our readers the whispered sentences, so pleasant to the utterers, so foolish to all others. They were not quite so free from observation in their walk as they thought themselves. Behind a clump of flowering shrubs which concealed a gate leading into a lane that skirted the grounds, a figure crouched and was completely hidden by the foliage; quiet and stealthily as a cat, and with an animal gleam in the keen eyes, the watcher observed the youthful pair, gaining all that the eye unaided by the ear could gather, for the conversation was in too low tone, for any word, save that of "week," to reach the spy.

Presently a servant came with a shawl and a message, "Master thinks the air is getting chilly, Miss Gertrude."

"That's a hint for us to return to the house," said Gertrude, as the shawl was wrapped round her by Bernard, and in a few moments more they left the garden, and in less than an hour's time the young man was walking briskly the two miles that separated Chiswick, the home of his affianced wife, from Brompton, the metropolitan suburb where Bernard Traice for the present resided. What a glow was in his heart, how buoyant with delight he felt. The present seemed absorbed in the blissful future, visions of a little cottage nestling among the trees of Fulham arose before him and one beloved form and face made the light, and joy, and gladness thereof. So rapt was he in this contemplation, that he knocked at his door, and entered his lodgings mechanically, as much asleep as it regarded the actual, as any sonnambulist, when a letter on his table caught his eye. He opened it listlessly, but in an instant what a change! For a moment his face flushed scarlet to the very temples, and then the blood receded, leaving even his lips white. With knit brow and clenched teeth he reads on. Some drops of cold perspiration started on his forehead, and relieved the sense of suffocation. The letter is not long, but he reads it again and again, as if bewilderment succeeded to his first agony. Yet the words were plain enough :—

"Mr. Bernard Traice,—I have found you out at length, and know all about you. Your office, your abode, your intended, are all known to me. Do not think to escape me again. My claims on you must be, and shall be settled, before you form your new ties. I thought of going this evening to Mr. Peck, and telling him the Dublin history of the worthy his granddaughter is about to marry. If Jessie had been with me, I would, but as it is, I warn you to come without delay to No. — Dacre Street, Westminster, second floor, and make what reparation you can, or dread the consequences. Your deceived and injured. Annie ———.''

"Deceived and injured!" muttered Bernard through his clenched teeth—"Oh fool, wretched fool that I have been," he added, striking his clenched hand on the marble mantel-piece, without feeling the pain of the bruise. He rang the bell, and in answer to his inquiries, learned that the letter had been left only a quarter of an hour before he returned. "Are you ill, sir?" said the maid-servant, startled out of her routine manners by his pallid looks.

"No! oh, no! Betsy, I am going out some distance, and must be late. Ask Mrs. Thrifton for the loan of her latch key."

"Certainly, Sir, missus will have no sort of objection to *your* having of the key," said the girl with an emphasis that implied an unusual favour was granted.

In a few minutes Bernard Traice was walking towards town. He hailed each passing omnibus, but to his annoy-ance they were all full, and his impatience was compelled to submit to a foot pace, until he reached Knightsbridge, where he jumped into a cab, and told the driver the direction. Of course the man bungled in finding it, and there was more than the usual excuse; for Dacre Street was amid a knot of turnings in the most populous part of the ancient city of Westminster. The improvements that have razed the wretched lanes and alleys that used to be the haunts of filth and crime, under the shadow of the magnificent western front of the Abbey, has spared Dacre Street; and the dwel-lings there, mostly good-sized houses fallen into decay, and now occupied by a very different class from those for whom they were built, are crowded by a motley tribe, of whom the labourer, living by honest toil, forms only a very small fraction.

The cab, after many inquiries and much loss of time, stopped at an archway, out of which an open door led into the passage of a spacious gloomy house. While Bernard's hand was on the knocker, a woman odorous of gin, holding a flaring candle in her hand, stepped from the side parlour, and said, "Is it Mrs. Moriarty you're wanting, Sir ?   I don't think she's within at this present, but I'll see in a jiffy."

Meanwhile, as Bernard heard the flap of ragged slippers, and the trail of the draggling gown, as the woman ascended the filthy stairs, he groaned in spirit at the mortification of being there.   He had but little time to arrange his thoughts, for a voice, that he knew too well, was sounding on the stairs, and " Walk up, Sir," was the invitation.

"No," said the young man, "I must trouble Mrs. Moriarty to come down."

Persisting in his refusal, at length a tall, tawdry woman, approaching middle age, holding a handkerchief to her eyes to conceal the tears she did *not* shed, descended to the passage.

"I am glad," said Bernard, "that you have your bonnet on, for I must see you for a few minutes outside."

"Outside !   Where ?   For goodness' sake, come up stairs. We can't talk on business on the street."

"Anywhere but under a roof with you."

And so, as he continued obstinate, forth they went.   Just under the lamp-post at the corner, a young man, turning short round from the street to the door, struck against Bernard and knocked his hat off.   "I beg your pardon," was the hasty apology, followed by the surprised exclamation, and a quick glance at his companion, "Why, Traice ! is it you, here?"   "Yes, Fred, a matter of—of—business," he stammered out.   Indeed ! well, I've a patient here ;" and the young surgeon with a puzzled look entered the house. Bernard, bursting with vexation, out-walked his companion, who, coming up out of breath, said, "Let us cross the broadway into the Park."   Her suggestion was followed, and there in the birdcage walk the wretched, entrapped youth heard the proposals of the harpy at his side.

"Money, money—and yet more money—or exposure !" That was the sum and substance of her conversation.

In vain Bernard spoke of the money he had given years before to put her in a shop.

"I was unfortunate in business," she said.   In vain he pleaded poverty.

"You have a good appointment in a government office." In vain he said he could afford no more.

" You can afford to marry."

Yes, money, money, a sum down, two hundred pounds, and she would go to America—she and Jessie. If not, she would go to Mr. Peck without delay. To give her a five-pound note, and to promise that he would see her in that place on the following evening to effect a settlement, if possible, was the only alternative that presented itself to Bernard.

"And all this," said he, as he paced with heavy steps towards his home, " arises from one mad drinking bout,—how little did I think of the consequences of what, in my sin and folly, I called a frolic."

In the course of his walk, he saw all around him evidences of the vice he deplored. There were the flaring lamps of the gin-palace, the illuminated clock—the only true thing in that temple of lies—recording the hours the drunkard wasted. There were bloated men reeling out, whose mouths were open sepulchres; and women, with nothing left of womanhood but the capacity of suffering; and worse still, if worse could be, there were children hanging by the tattered garments of their parents, or clinging to breasts so withered and hardened, and seared by liquid fire, that the very stones in the streets were tender in comparison. What could perdition show more horrible than these crowds vomited out of these glaring drinkeries?

"And I, wretch that I was, fell into this odious vice—became like these loathsome creatures! Fool! I'm justly punished."

As remorse thus lashed him with a whip of scorpions, he came upon another and very different throng. From the door of a hall a decent company were dispersing. There was shaking of hands and friendly farewells, and a comfortable look of being at ease in body and mind manifested by most. While in others an earnest, thoughtful, resolute manner, showed men engaged in some work that roused and elevated them.

"You gave them some home truths to-night, M'Ure," said an old man as he walked by the side of a tall, strong, florid, middle-aged man, who was wiping his ample forehead, while his chest heaved with lingering excitement.

"Home truths, man! Why, if I was silent, the very stones would rise up and testify against me. Temperance has been God's truth to me: it has given me back my wife, my children, my home—all, dear, holy, human love—that drink had banished. Aye, and more than that! Why, friend! you know it took me from the mouth of the pit, and put me in the way of hearing how to scale the mount of God. And can I be silent?"

"Never!" replied the old man—catching the other's enthusiasm—"never! You, and such as you, M'Ure, who have known the sting of the serpent, are the best to warn others. Yes, and to win as well as warn. Go on, and God speed you." So saying, he knocked at the door of his comfortable dwelling, and the companions separated.

Bernard Traice had heard every word, and his self-reproach gave added power to the testimony. With a wistful gaze he looked after M'Ure, as he turned from the main road, and quickened his pace homeward, and, "Oh, that my heart was like that man's!" was his wish as the stalwart form receded from his sight.

At length, poor Traice entered his dwelling. Less than three hours had elapsed since he had first returned full of hope; and now worried, anxious, and alarmed, he laid his throbbing head upon the pillow, wondering, in the strong revulsion of his feelings, whether there was any one so wretched as himself. For where to get the money required to effect his release from his miserable entanglement was a problem he knew not how to solve.

Yet Bernard Traice was no hardened libertine, no coarse voluptuary. He had lost both parents in his early boyhood; and an uncle, who resided in Dublin, had been at the charge of his education. At an early age, the youth had entered the University, and, for a considerable time, naturally expected to be his uncle's heir—was led to this expectation by his uncle's own words. Unhappily there could not be a worse guide for an orphan than this same uncle, for he was a pompous, weak, self-indulgent man, always saying fine sentiments and doing foolish actions. "Bernard, my boy!" he would exclaim as he sat over his wine, "I recorded a vow at my sister's grave—your sainted mother!—that I'd be a father to you, and, by Jove, you may depend on Terence O'Flaherty keeping his word. He'd scorn to do less. Though the expense of College is beyond all reasonable computation entirely."

Bernard knew his uncle's mode of exaggeration, and used to smile or joke in reply, though often the constant reminder that he was a dependent was a sort of perpetual blister to the youth, who meanwhile studied hard, and hoped to make his education a means of emancipation from the humiliation of his position. He saw and felt no good home influence, and though no one was more eloquent in praise of gentlemanly moderation and gentlemanly honour than his uncle, yet as those praises were uttered over the wine cup or the whisky punch, and were accompanied with all sorts of wild stories of revelry, it was no wonder that they were as sounding brass or a tinkling cymbal—noise, and nothing more.

Glad, indeed, was Bernard, when, at the age of eighteen, he got permission in the long vacation to visit his father's relations in England. He stayed his full time of ten weeks, not feeling particularly uneasy at receiving no replies to his letters, for he knew his uncle did not like letter-writing, when his return was hastened by a dirty scrap of a letter from Pat Casey, the old man-servant, who wrote—

"Your honor had better make haste, or you'll be too late, sorrow on it, for the important evint. And its many a salt tear myself has been shedding for the master in this ixthremity, for his rason is lost entirely, and the use of his limbs, barring the crutches, which he stuck to, and its sad at heart I am dear! that he ever laned to any other support, for his weakness has desaved him, and may be the strength of the drop too, and has led to this bitter ind of a beginning of sorrow for us all.

"So, for the love of your sowl make haste and relave the watching, and weeping, of your faithful

"PAT CASEY."

That his uncle was dangerously ill, was the only clear idea that Bernard gained from this note, and so, with all speed, he set off, and arrived at his uncle's house in Rathmines Road, just in time to witness—the return from a funeral? No, a wedding! The old man had ended his orations on gentlemanly conduct by marrying his maid-servant. This event, of course, altered Bernard's prospects completely. The aged bridegroom, already ashamed of his folly, went out of town, and the youth, hurt and irritated, returned to College.

The tempter is always near, and, in an evil hour, Bernard mingled with a party of reckless young men, who determined to have their revenge for the long time that the youth had held aloof from them.   They plied the novice with the mad-dening draught till reason and conscience slept, till manhood was degraded and brutehood exalted, and the youth recovered from his "spree" to find himself not only sick and wretched, but entangled in the snares of a designing woman, years older than himself, and well versed in all the crooked ways that vice lays open for the footsteps of folly.   The vices are certainly social.   They assail a man in companies ; and in-temperance (let shrinking, time-serving moralists cloak the matter as they may), is the surest guide to those of whom inspired wisdom says—"Her feet go down to death, her steps take hold on hell :" "Her house is the way to hell, going down to the chambers of death."

From that miserable time, as long as Bernard was a stu-dent, he had not a moment's peace.   This woman, for some reason best known to herself, wished to coax or threaten him into a marriage.   She represented herself as a respectable widow, and had the effrontery to call herself the victim of the wretched youth she pursued.   Bernard was reserved, both by natural temperament and from principle, and as he had no near friend to whom he could carry the sore burden of his aching heart, he shrunk from displaying this plague spot of his soul to a mere casual companion, so he bore the heavy yoke, he had put upon his shoulders, alone.   Every valuable that affection had bestowed upon him in days gone by, was sold to make up money to buy off the mercenary woman who beset him.   For a time she gave him a respite of some months, and he began to hope that he should hear no more of her, when she suddenly appeared, to Bernard's unutterable dismay, with a new and innocent claimant on his attention. This made him take a decided step.   He would inherit a little property from his father on coming of age—a small freehold.   He borrowed money on this of an accommodating usurer, who gained a large fortune by helping young men on the road to ruin.   With the sum thus gained he purchased the promise of Mrs. Moriarty that she would molest him no more ; and when he avoided one of the busy thoroughfares of Dublin, which was very near the College, he did so with some degree of satisfaction, for his tormentor had established herself in a cigar shop there, and was certainly fitly placed, if weeds should go together.

Relieved so far—but still feeling the stings of the inward monitor—he passed his examination, came to England, and, by the influence of a gentleman who was indignant at the old uncle's folly, obtained a post of no very great emolument in one of the government offices. It was not equal to what, from education, he might have aspired to, but the secret sorrow of his youth had made him humble.

Four years passed; he had regained his peace of mind in the only way in which a wounded spirit can obtain healing —by penitence and prayer. A year before our story opens, he was boating on the Thames and saved the life of an aged gentleman whose wherry was run down and capsized by a steamer. The watermen had hard work to save themselves in the rapid current, and their employer must have perished but for the strong swimming and sturdy grasp of Bernard, who had not breasted the waves in the bay of Dublin from his boyhood for nothing.

Such a service, rendered and received, of course led to intimacy. Mr. Peck was a worthy, but a very cautious man, and nothing but the great obligation he was under to Bernard would have opened his door to a stranger in such a familiar manner. A genuine native of the great city, he had all a Londoner's reserve, not to say suspicion. But Bernard Traice's claim was paramount. The family comprised Miss Peck, an elderly young lady, the old man's eldest daughter, and Gertrude Williams, the orphan child of his younger daughter.

Now, Miss Priscilla Peck, or "aunt Prissy," as she was called by Gertrude, had not only a general dislike and disapproval of all such follies as courtship and marriage, but she was very ambitious for her niece, whom she loved as lonely hearts often love some one object—with a clutching, nervous, spasmodic love, that tormented rather than comforted its object. A naturally sweet temper, a good education, and better still, good principles, had counteracted the harassing caprices of the aunt, and so Gertrude diffused an

F

atmosphere of love around her, and was the light and music of the dwelling to both grandfather and aunt. When this accident occurred—a double accident indeed, for, to use old-fashioned words, Gertude fell over head and ears in love, as deeply as her grandfather fell into the river; and Bernard reversed his conduct, for he did not help *her* out. How could he, poor fellow? Was he not struggling in the same high tide, borne onward by the same strong current? To do them justice, Gertrude called her feelings gratitude, and Bernard called his admiration—and these were right names in the beginning; but Miss Peck was right when she said to her father, "One must be as blind and as hard as the monument" (a country woman would have said, "a mole or a bat," but Miss Peck was town bred) "not to see how this affair will end. It all comes, father, of you liking that horrid wherry. The young man saved your life, to be sure, and we're very much obliged to him, but if it ends in his wanting the life of this house, father, what are we to do then? and he only a clerk, or a something under government." "Pshaw! Prissy, folly! and yet, if I suspected such a thing, I'd—I'd do something: yes! something decisive. But don't let us commit ourselves. The youth is a good youth, certainly— and a first-rate swimmer."

This state of things could not last long. There came explanations, and refusals, and scoldings, and tears, and at length a reluctant consent, amounting almost to hostility in the aunt, and that kept the grandfather from being exactly cordial. However, this was gradually wearing away. The pleasant reflection that Gertrude would not go far from them —a pretty cottage among the trees of Fulham, not very far from Chiswick, having been selected — and the generous request made by Bernard, and which Gertrude, in the enthusiasm of her love tried to overrule, that her little fortune should be settled on herself, all reconciled them; and now the day was fixed, and Miss Peck was grand as the referee on all muslin and silk debates, and was consoling herself with the thought of how she would arrange the house against the return from the wedding tour, when the terrible storm that threatened to sweep away all his prospects gathered and loomed near, unseen by all but the wretched Bernard.

He had expended his ready money in the necessary preparations for entering on housekeeping, reserving only what
would be needed for his wedding tour. For the first time, he
resolved to write to his uncle and borrow a sum of money,
though that was but a forlorn hope, for the poor man had
had plenty of time to discover that there is no domestic
despot so pitiless and exacting as a vulgar simpleton. However, to write was a relief, it was a putting off of the evil
day. How tedious were the dismal hours! How constrain-
ed, how guilty, he felt as he stood with his load of secret
anxiety in the presence of Gertrude! Those frank, blue eyes,
that open brow, how in their innocent confidence they reproached him. She saw that he was ill at ease. It would
take a far better dissembler than Bernard to conceal his
anxiety from the glance of alarmed affection. It was quite
true that he had a headache, and that must suffice as the
reason. For the first time, as Bernard left the villa he felt a
sense of relief. He was glad the night was stormy; and as
he rode to town, and kept his dreary appointment in St.
James's Park, desperation compelled him to say,—"If I can
borrow the money, well, you shall have it, if not, do your
worst, I care not, I cannot be more wretched than you have
made me," and so they parted. Whether the wretched
woman thought her victim likely to escape her, she muttered
something about she would wait four days, and then, if the
money was not forthcoming for her to sail in the next mail
steamer, she would expose him, that she would. She would
confront him, even at the altar.

For those four days, Bernard scarcely ate or slept. Once
on the Sabbath-day, that intervened, he determined to throw
himself at the feet of Mr. Peck, and confess the sin of his
youth; but when he approached to do so, Miss Peek was
there, and both the opportunity and the resolution passed
away.

It was Wednesday; he left his office, having obtained
leave for three weeks—very unlike a happy bridegroom he
looked, for no answer had come to his letter; he rode to his
lodgings, but hastened away, fearing the intrusion of his foe.
The sun was shining brightly, and all nature looked gay as
he passed over the green, and down the lane he knew so well.

As he entered the side-gate referred to, and that was ofte
left open, he looked behind him along the path he had traced,
and thought he saw the dreaded form in the distance.   The
pathetic words of Scripture rushed to his lips, "Hast thou
found me again?   Oh, mine enemy!"   In great disorder, he
locked the gate and entered the little parlour where he had
spent so many happy hours.   Gertrude was sitting on a
stool at her grandfather's feet, holding his withered hand in
hers, and looking up with filial love into his face, as if mutely
thanking him for all the care he had taken of her childhood
—a gilded and silken book, a present, lay upon her lap—
open.   Bernard's eye fell upon the words—

> "It is an anxious happiness,
>   It is a fearful thing,
> When first the maiden's gentle hand
>   Puts on the wedding ring.
>
> She passeth from her father's house,
>   Unto a stranger's care;
> And who can tell what mighty change,
>   What griefs may wait her there?"

A spasm shot through him as he read—he rallied after a
moment.   "Never," he said, "by God's help, Gertrude,
shall any care or grief, that I can avert, await you; but"—
he faltered

"I believe it, Bernard! I believe it," said the grandfather,
more warmly than he was wont, and grasping the young
man's hand, he united Gertrude's with it.   There was a ring
at the bell, and Bernard started and trembled like a leaf—a
minute passed in silence.   When the door opened, he expected nothing less than to see his pursuer enter, particularly as he heard a sort of confused call in the distance, and
the maid rushed rather than walked in.   "Oh, please, come,
Mr. Traice. You, Sir, are best, for the gardener's fallen down
in a fit at the gate."

In a moment, Bernard's presence of mind returned, and
he followed the maid and helped to raise the poor fellow,
almost envying him the brief repose of insensibility.   The
man breathed heavily, struggled, opened his eyes, and looked
wildly round.

"Where is she?" he exclaimed.

"Whom?" said Bernard.

"My wife—that ever I should call her so!"

"Your wife? Are you a married man?"

"What are you talking about?" said the maids, who, joined by Miss Peck, came crowding round the man. A light broke in on Bernard's brain, and he said gently, "You had better leave him till he gathers strength."

"This must be explained," said Miss Peck, walking away, and the maids were both busy, saying, as they followed, "I had a glimpse,—a tall woman in a green gown, mem."

"Compose yourself, my good fellow," said Bernard.

"Thank'ee, Sir, I'll go speak to master, he knows my misfortune," gasped the man, rising and tottering to the parlour. "She's found me, Sir!" exclaimed the man. "She! Who?"

"My wife, as I told you about, Sir. She was at the gate when I answered the ring; though," he added—considering, "she didn't seem to expect to see me neither, for I think as my knees gave way under me with the fright, I saw her flying off. Oh, Sir, I must go, I can never be here to be haunted by that woman."

"Why, Tomlins! said Bernard eagerly—"Is she so bad?"

"Bad! Sir. I was left a widower, with two sweet children, and as good a bit of nursery ground, as any in Fulham, when I fell in with this body who came to manage my place. I loved a drop of drink, and that was my ruin. She saw my folly and helped me on, till I gave her a wife's name and place in my house, and then she spent and wasted until she got me out of house and home. But that was nothing to her ill usage of my poor children. They both died. Ah! Sir, the law don't say she killed 'em, but I say by neglect she let 'em die. Then, when all was spent, she left me and went to Dublin, to follow her old ways of shame and deceit —after a year she wrote and promised amendment, and came to me; but after plaguing me for six months, she went away, taking my poor sister's baby with her. My sister died when the poor thing was but a month old. What she wanted to encumber herself with an infant for, I know not; I fear it wasn't for good; and from that time, till I saw her at the gate, I've never clapped eyes on her. Master knows all, but Miss Peck arn't been told, for it's a dismal story;

and I ask pardon of Miss Gertrude for bringing my troubles before her; but I was so took to, that I'm mazed-like."

It is needless, nay, it would be impossible to describe the feelings with which Bernard listened. How completely the incubus fell off, for, of course, his deepest anguish was the thought that there really was a living being, the evidence of his sin, who had a real claim on him: in the midst of his own agitation, he ventured to say—"Rely on it, she did not expect to see you—her flight proves that."

Early that evening Bernard wrote to Mrs. Tomlins, No. —— Dacre Street, and said merely these words :—

"Your husband will not be molested—his master knows your history, and forbids your troubling him. If you want to make any reparation for the misery you have caused, inform your husband where the child you call Jessie, his niece, is. Answer this to John Tomlins, or to Mr. Steele, solicitor, at —— Street, Strand."

That night, before he slept, Bernard Traice wrote a pledge of total abstinence in his pocket-book, and signed it. He had long been a water drinker, but he wished to make assurance doubly sure, and in all respects to begin a new life the next day. He prayed for strength, and his prayer was heard.

The wedding passed off pleasantly—it was a quiet rather than a gay affair—for Gertrude shrunk from much display, and her grandfather could not bear the excitement of a great party.

When they returned from their wedding tour, Gertrude said, as they took possession of their pretty house, "Tell me, dearest, why you thought it necessary to sign the pledge?" Bernard answered, "Because, love, I made 'a stumble on the threshold' of manhood that might, and but for heavenly mercy would, have ruined my entire career;" and then, with manly blushes for the past, he told her the story of his sin, and its long and bitter punishment.

Nothing remains to be added, but that Tomlins received a certificate of the burial of poor little Jessie, the innocent impostor, and that Bernard found out M'Ure, and became active in helping him to spread the safe, sure plan, of total abstinence.

UPS AND DOWNS OF LIFE.

"Take thy beak from out my heart,
Take thy shadow from my floor.
Quoth the Raven—'Nevermore.'"

EDGAR POE.

"WELL, friends, may you be as prosperous in this house as your predecessors, the Minton's, were. They had not, at the outset, your prospects, and yet they made a fortune here."

"Thank you, Sir! but I hope we shall do better than they did, for, after all, they were but earth-worms—mere money grubs."

This remark and reply were made across a table, where decanters and glasses sparkled, and at which three persons were seated. An elderly, clerical looking gentleman, who had uttered the above wish as he sipped his wine, the others a newly married couple, and as comely a pair as the eye need crave to look on.

A certain maiden aunt of ours, who has a perverse habit of asserting that there are not ten per cent. of real marriages out of all the matrimonial compacts that take place, would assuredly have admitted this couple to be a well matched pair, really and truly married—formed to meet by nature and reason, love and truth. The bride had not only the sprightliest little form, and merriest face that ever adorned and cheered a dwelling, but there was intelligence as well as mirth in her clear, blue eyes, health and industry in her "household motions light and free," and if the little saucy nose indicated, to a physiognomist, a temper rather sudden; yet the benevolence of the open brow gave a guarantee that sullenness and obstinacy were unknown. The husband of this little piece of witchery was a young man of a fine presence, and very quiet demeanour, looking in consequence older than his real age, which, in truth, was less than that of his juvenile looking wife.   John Waverton was one of those people, who, without the least assumption, always command respect. The stamp of superiority was on the manner of all he said and did.   The world smiled on them, a handsome druggist's shop in one of the leading thoroughfares of the Metropolis was their abode.   The business was old and well established, and had, as already intimated, enabled the former occupant to make a fortune.   John Waverton and his only brother had inherited a handsome sum on the demise of their father, a farmer in Essex; the farm went to the elder son, and as soon as John, the younger, came of age, his capital was invested in the purchase of the business where he had served his apprenticeship.   He had only his own inclinations to consult in the choice of a wife, and a young lady, an orphan, being on a visit to a neighbour, the acquaintance commenced, which ended in the young tradesman making his establishment complete, by putting a wife there as lady-president. And though his elder brother, and only relative, would have been quite as well pleased if the young lady had added to the account at the banker's—yet John said truly, and most people, even without his predilections, would echo the senti- ment, " The best dower a wife can have, is that which money can never bestow or compensate—Nature's wealth."   So Shakspere's adage—" The course of true love never did run smooth," was not true of them, the marriage bells were not more harmonious than the inner and outer life of John and Maria Waverton.

It was natural to their age, station, and circumstances, that there should be merry makings and parties in abundance when the bride came home; and as the wedding took place late in the autumn, there was the winter season " quite con- vaniant," as the Irish housemaid said, for festive meetings. So there were parties for the older of their acquaintance, and, of course, they had a large circle—(prosperous people always have)—" good substantial dinners," " real hospitable affairs," praised and quoted with great gusto, by those who, having arrived at a solid period of life, love to manifest their solidity in feeding at all events.   Then there were charming evening parties for the young friends of the newly married pair, where mirth and music, fun and frolic, finery and flirting, kept company with wine and cake, negus and trifle, nuts and noyeau. Oh, never were married pair so popular as John Waverton and his fair Maria.

But, in a large visiting list, there are always some who dislike parties, and those are often the most sensible people of your acquaintance. Now little Mrs. Waverton's good nature was on the alert to please these also; and in addition to very particular female friends, who ran in when they pleased out of pity to her inexperience "just to advise the poor dear,"—there was Mr. Ignatius Von Deep, an elderly gentleman of British birth, but German descent, who, as a man of marvellous learning, and profound mind, was not only the oldest friend but the oracle of the house. This gentleman, the descendant of a long line of Lutheran ministers, had himself been educated with a view to the pastoral office, but his penetration detected certain errors in the doctrines in which he had been reared, and he, as in duty bound, changed his creed; but still he found flaws and defects— sometimes in doctrine, sometimes in discipline—and he changed again and again, until having made a complete circuit he found all were wrong, but himself, and with this comfortable conviction he settled himself mostly as a hearer where a man of great talent preached, and amused his leisure by regularly taking to pieces the discourse, much to the edification of all who loved argument, of the find-fault kind. Mr. Von Deep soon had many allies: among them were John Waverton's former master and predecessor and his wife, though it was difficult to say why they liked the "philosopher" as they styled him; unless it was that whenever a collection was made for any religious object, he always found out some moral and conscientious scruple against giving, and as they loved money they said "what a conclusive reasoner Mr. Von Deep is:" a chair in their house, a pipe and glass, and, what was better than all, listeners, were generally ready. By degrees, it grew into a custom that he came, and as among his other pursuits he was a Lecturer on Chemistry, he was able to patronize their shop sometimes. Young Waverton had therefore grown up in the firm conviction that Mr. Von Deep was the best and wisest of men; and this sincere conviction expressed itself so legibly on his countenance and in his actions that it is no wonder the distinguished individual in question patronized the young man, and allowed himself to feel as deep an interest about his welfare as it was rational a philosopher should feel in any mere mundane affair whatever. Nay, though he looked on courtship and marriage as a weakness, and always quoted Lord Bacon's remark:

"Great spirits and great business do keep out this weak passion,"

yet he so far condescended as to examine the qualifications of Maria in the cooking department, and finding that she not only understood that, but mixed wine punch to perfection; after partaking, before her marriage, of some of her manufacture one evening, he took his pipe from his mouth, puffed out as much smoke as did duty for a flourish of trumpets, and exclaimed "You have my consent, my boy!—Marry soon!—First rate!" Whether the latter eulogium referred to the punch or the lady was uncertain, but young Waverton, of course, took the advice (when it pleases them, people always do) ; and at the opening of our story, Mr. Von Deep was uttering his daily wish for the prosperity of the pair, over his port-wine negus.

Poor Maria! who could blame her, that among her little feminine weaknesses was a pride in her household management. It was not only very pardonable, but, under right direction, very laudable. Rely upon it, fair reader, your husband will sooner pardon a tasteless combination in your best piece of Berlin wool-work, than a tasteless combination for his dinner. If your music is out of time it will not plague him half so much as his meals being behind time; and your very neatest French translation will go for nothing compared with those neat translations that

"Gar auld claes look amaist as weel's the new."

But poor Maria was ambitious; she wished to excel all other wives in the house and table department; and she forgot that economy is the only sure basis of liberality. How industrious she was! brewing her own beer. "Other people bought theirs, and wretched adulterated stuff it was,"—now she made hers, and it was genuine,—"certainly the brewing utensils and altering the wash-house, by building a brewing copper, made a great dip in thirty pounds," "but they should save that in time," "besides drinking the real thing?" and, certainly, if by rapid consumption the brewing utensils were to be paid for, what with the two young men in the shop, the errand boy, and the two maids, all of whom were to be kept fat and healthy on the capital home-brewed, there was little doubt the difficult arithmetical problem was sure to be solved.

Then Maria had quite a genius for home-made wines.— Her pickles and preserves were very good, but "*Excelsior*" was the motto over her home-made wine bin, and it was, as years went on, a treat she often gave herself to bring out her Damson wine, and after her visitors drank their port, to entreat them to try it, and hear them declare, as in duty bound, that it was not only equal to the foreign vintage, but superior (and really if all stories be true about damaged cider, logwood, molasses, brandy, and alum for crust, being the fine compound sold as port, perhaps they were right). Then as to champagne, the spirit of honest English gooseberries defied and triumphed over it—though it was always found that the visitors' curiosity and wonder were so excited at this marvel, they were obliged to drink a great deal of the the foreigner to establish the natural triumph. Maria would certainly have tried her hand at distilling if she had not been hampered with certain legal difficulties. However, she was a good customer to the distiller; who, if the truth must be told, really did more for her wine in the way of strength (and wickedness) than the poor innocent fruit ever effected.

Mr. Von Deep was the patron and referee on all questions, not merely of metaphysics, but physics; and under his tutelage, John Waverton became quite gifted in the way of argument,—as a listener! Maria, who had been religiously educated, would have liked to have gone regularly to an adjacent place of worship, but her husband could not listen to "the poor stuff" preached there; so, with Mr. Von Deep, he went on an exploring expedition, but rarely returned satisfied, and never enough so to determine on settling down as a hearer. When there were notabilities to be heard, and Mr. Von Deep scented them out as a crow does carrion, and invited Waverton to hear them, then he would come out great in taking to pieces their discourse,—if they were popular, he proved that no profound man ever could be popular. —If, and it was often the case, they were wandering clouds, rather than stars, and enveloped their hearers in mist, he called them profound, but showed how much profounder he himself was, by finding out—"they should have put the case quite differently;" or "they were not sound;" or, more frequently still, "they were not original"—there being no originality that he, Mr. Von Deep, had not preconceived. And thus, not merely months but years passed,—not without strong traces of their flight. Children were born in rather quick succession, and in truth were neither healthy nor good-tempered, beautiful they certainly were as to form and features, but fractious, restless little mortals, that tortured their mother, tried their father, and tormented their nurse. All the drugs in the shop, and many of them were tried, could not, as their nurse said, make them happy children.

Somehow, with all Maria Waverton's management, things went wrong perpetually. No one was ever so victimised by servants. The number of lazy, dishonest women, who dared to enter that house was amazing. And as to modesty and sobriety, the qualities were unknown. An Irish housemaid was the only girl who kept aloof from the young men in the shop. Then, some tippled quietly in large quantities and escaped detection for a long time; others drank less and openly, and were soon exposed and discharged. Then, in seven years, there had been three criminal trials of the young men in the shop for defrauding their master, and the fourth case, much the worst, was allowed to escape, for John Waverton was ashamed of having another prosecution against his assistants. The only faithful servant who had eaten their bread, was the porter lad, and he was crotchety, never tasted the home-brewed, preferred money to beer, and was not popular in either the house or shop; but yet did his work so well that he had been put behind the counter during one of the hurricanes that shook off some rotten leaves from the business tree; and once there, he had worked, and studied, until Waverton reluctantly admitted to himself he could not do without him.

At the end of seven years, how fared it with the heads of the household? Changed! changed! something—it could not be tears, for they had had no heavy heart troubles—had quenched the beaming light in Maria's blue eyes, and they looked dull and fishy; her complexion, instead of being a clear, pink-tinted white, kindling into vermillion on the cheeks and lips, was a pale yellow tipped with purple. The elastic roundness of the slender form had departed, and left an angular, stooping frame of bones, that no amount of dressing and decorating could make look anything but wiry and hard, and there was worry and vexation not only on the face, but in every gesture, and most of all in the thin, high, shrewish voice. If John Waverton ever looked at her, and recalled what she had been, no wonder if he sang :—

> "All that's bright must fade,
> The brightest still the fleetest."

but, perhaps, he never did notice the change, it had gone on day by day, and like an encroaching sea that creeps on, wave by wave, tide by tide, is not observed until it obliterates the old boundary. So his wife's beauty and good temper departed. And he, too, was changed—less outwardly than inwardly. He had still the same tall, manly form and regular features, but his quietness had gradually become apathy, the calm of the serene brow was now a heavy gloom. Mr. Von Deep himself did not smoke so much, nor, indeed, did he drink so much. That philosophic tutor had the advantage of change of scene and persons, going about and drinking at other people's tables, and that caused a ripple in the puddle of his existence. True, like a puddle, he exhaled putrid vapours, most noxious to all within his range, yet still there was movement in him; but John Waverton's life grew stagnant, the mildew of inertia deposited itself like a crust over him. His nervous and mercurial little wife said truly enough, "he wanted rousing," and, if domestic annoyances, bad debts, a failing trade, fretful children, and it must be added, a scolding wife, could have roused him, he need not have wanted any stimulus they could supply. But, unfortunately, he was past that. His constant pipe, and his capital home-brewed, and his refresher of whisky and bitters before dinner, and his afternoon negus, and his courtesy glasses at odd times with customers, and his nightly quietus of grog, his "Night Cap," as he called it, were sedatives that defied all antidotes.

Maria, always at work, managing, compounding, finding fault, fidgeting, fuming, was, of course, both weak and feverish; and cordials without end—some said to be cooling, and others stimulating, and all with a high character, were the habit, and became the necessity of her existence. She could not get through her tough daily wrestle with the wild surge of annoyances without them. Now, dear reader, do not say, "Oh! this man was a confirmed drunkard, and his wife no better." *I tell you that neither of them were drunkards*, as the world rates drunkenness. No one, not their worst enemy would have whispered the word in reference to them. Waverton was noted as a "steady, highly respectable man —a little too quiet, perhaps." And his opinion, whenever he could be induced to give it, was always most highly valued. His wife, too, what ceaseless, untiring, activity! "Quite a Martha," Mr. Von Deep said. Drunkards, indeed! Preposterous slander! Who ever saw them the worse for ———? Oh! the thought was abominable.

Some satirist has said, "Our morals depend on the state of our stomach;" and this is quite true as to inebriation— the filthy, brawling nuisance, whom policemen drag before a tribunal, and charge with drunkenness—as far as *quantity* of drink is concerned, consumes far less than the magistrate who reprimands and fines him. The servant girl who loses her character, and gets turned into the streets to perish, body and soul, never did, or could, drink the half that her genteel, respectable mistress, by long habit and medical prescription, can take with impunity. It is an empty stomach, poverty, destitution, ignorance, and desperation, that wise men often punish as drunkenness: while the great consumers are— "all honourable men!" Do you doubt it? Look at the keeper of yon low beer shop. You turn up your nose at the immoral vulgarian. Look at the brewer who makes the drink that the other sells. "Oh, worthy gentleman! he shall represent our town in Parliament,—he shall preside at our Bible meeting,—he shall devise a plan for bettering the condition of the poor; and we'll shout ourselves hoarse in his praise."

Well, sustaining many a shake, for his business was firmly rooted, and could not be easily plucked up, Waverton sipped and smoked and dosed through another seven years: and then the accumulated expenses and losses, and bills and mortgages, could be dammed up and kept back no longer, and ruin came like a flood bearing all before it—sweeping away everything but the miserable wretches who, helpless, aimless, and, alas! numerous, for there were five children, stood staring in stupefaction at the desolation around them.

"But surely they had friends?" Their friends loved their table and not them; and that being gone, the bond of union was dissolved. Indeed, these it was who said, "What folly of the Wavertons to be giving their champagne dinners!" "How unprincipled! living above their means." "Poor Waverton!" said another, with insolent compassion, "he got into a false position;" while Mr. Von Deep entered into an argument, to prove that "the age was false and wrong altogether,—all shams and lies, and no man could get into a right position. He had always told Waverton so, but it did him no good. However, he was sorry, sincerely sorry." And, perhaps, as he lost most, he was the chief mourner over the downfall—of the dinners.

Meanwhile, poor Maria took her children to a mean cottage at Bayswater, while their father was in the Queen's Bench prison. And here, by the sale of her few personal effects that had been allowed her by the creditors, she managed to exist; but the luxuriously fed children suffered terribly by the suddenly altered diet, they became thin and low-spirited. The elasticity of childhood was gone. One only, the eldest girl, and second child, had a strong vitality, and it showed itself in such outbreaks of temper to her brothers and sisters, such murmurings and mischief, that the tormented, jaded mother, resolved to send her to a neighbouring school, even if she starved herself to pay for it. So the young tyrant was transferred to a small private school—the school-room was close and hot; and the unusual atmosphere, combined with the altered diet of the once pampered child, led to fearful results. At the end of a week she fell ill of malignant scarlet fever, and, if it were a fictitious narrative we were writing, we should hesitate to tell the sequel; but truth, more strange and awful than fiction, compels the record, that in five days from the commencement of the fever all the children had died except the unfortunate and unpromising child who brought the malady among them. Suffering far more, apparently than the rest; yet—while the fine eldest boy gasped his last, and her two little sisters tossed their burning head upon their pillow, and in delirium sang themselves to sleep—the long last sleep of death, and her baby brother, little Tim! sobbed out his life on his mother's bosom, she lived on, insensible, yet alive. After many weeks she woke to consciousness, and found her father released from prison, cowering over the miserable fire; and her mother! could it be her mother? or one of the gibbering ghosts that had haunted her fever dreams? Yes, that blue, haggard, bony, tattered thing, was really her mother!

"Mamma! where are they all? Call them, I want them to play with me."

The child was interrupted by a cry, a shriek, that seemed to tear its way from the very heart of the wretched mother.

"Oh, dont child, you'll kill me if you ask me for them,—my babes, my pretty babes! Oh, dear, dear, I surely cannot die, nothing will kill me!" She walked up and down, palpitating and trembling in every nerve. Words are impotent to tell the misery of that home. Suffice it, that not only the fever left the patient, but the childhood left her also, and she recovered to be a withered-looking creature, prematurely old, but strong and wiry, and joyless. There are some natures misery makes selfish, and hers was one.

John Waverton retained, amid the wreck both of fortune and mind, one educational acquirement,—he wrote a very fine hand, and was, when he chose, a most skilful accountant, wretchedly as he had managed his own affairs; and his only relative, the elder brother before-named, as a last effort, procured a clerk's situation for him with a wine merchant; and on the day that poor Waverton entered on his new duties—

his late shopman and afore-time porter—the water drinker, concluded an agreement with the creditors (for whom he had conducted the capital old established business while the affairs had been winding up), and entered upon his own account as a master, the shop that, fourteen years before, he had been employed to sweep. Mr. Von Deep resolved to congratulate him, and was entering the shop for that purpose; but Miles Mettle, the new master, stopped him with —"'Take your shadow from my floor,' you obstruct the *sunshine*;" and somehow the old man, when he caught the look that accompanied the words, did not argue the question, but hobbled off, as fast as pride and gout would let him to his lonely home, where we may as well leave him to his fate—a cheating landlady, a drunken London nurse, and a neglected death-bed.

But John Waverton had not yet sounded the lowest deeps of misery. His luxurious life, his torpid system, all unfitted him for his new duties. Then both his wife and himself could better, as they said, do without eating than drinking. Refreshers and invigorators, and comforters, they must have. Wine was entirely beyond their means; but ale and spirits absorbed the salary of the poor clerk. No one, certainly, ever said he was drunk, but no one in their senses could say he was sober: and his dismissal came, for "Who," as his employer remarked, "could bear such a poverty-struck, dead-and-alive fellow?"

The little girl, being twelve years old, determined to escape the home miseries, and went to work at a dressmaker's, where she was half starved, and wholly perverted in temper and mind. The mother was ever either railing at her husband, or wailing for her children; the one spared to her being the least loved, and, as the innocent cause of the fever calamity, an object almost of dislike to her.

When Waverton's last chance failed, in a fit of rage his wife determined to take a situation, and hastened off to the doctor who had known her in better days, and who, out of gratitude or compassion, recommended her to an invalid lady who lived in great retirement at Chelsea, and was most quietly and respectably, in obedience to medical orders, drinking herself helpless and foolish. So away went Maria

G

Waverton, thinking herself not only the greatest martyr, but the noblest heroine that ever lived, and certainly well qualified to assist in keeping the patient from a too speedy recovery.

And then as John Waverton sat brooding in his lonely lodging, something rose within him, and stirred the depths of his nature. Station, credit, wife, children, all gone! Stolid and heavy as he had become, there was, unhappily for him, a latent tenderness yearning and throbbing in his heavy heart. Little faces seemed to crowd round him with beseeching eyes,—their imploring hands waved before him, —the stillness of his chamber seemed broken by hissing whispers and heavy sobs. He could bear it no longer,—he could not, dared not, be alone! His brain reeled, surely he was going mad! He rushed out; the air, and sounds of life recalled him for a time. It was evening—a calm evening —he wished it had been cloudy, tempestuous, for the serene moon and stars seemed awfully insensible to his agony. Suddenly he paused at the threshold of a place of worship, and though it was a week night, he saw people entering, and mechanically followed them. Was it in mercy or in judgment that his wearied form entered that sacred place? Alas! none can tell. The preacher in a solemn, earnest, yet plain, unpretending sermon, was speaking on the words—"Commit thy way unto the Lord, and he shall bring it to pass." The short pithy sentences were as the lightning flash that lights up a whole country for a brief moment with its lurid glare, —even so, doubtless, to the wretched man was the past brought fearfully and fully before him. Who can tell the dread spasm that shook his limbs, the flame that scorched his brain, as the demon of remorse began to rend him? A youth noticed him wiping big drops from his brow, and scanned him with a wondering, awe-struck eye. The congregation dispersed to their homes, many of them enjoying the peace "that passeth understanding." Where did poor Waverton go? On, and on, away from the busy streets, away out to the fields, with desperate haste, as if lashed on by fiends—over Kilburn meadows, over "Hampstead's breezy heath,"—on, on, to Hornsey wood: his blood is in a flame —strange lights flash before his eyes—wild sounds ring in his ears; there's a little still pond lies just before him, quiet as the night—cool, clear mirror of the silent stars! He can go no farther—his burning brain and panting heart shall rest here—yes, here!

Early next morning there were merry voices, and gay careering footsteps, resounding in the wood. Two boys were up and out for a ramble. On they bounded towards the pond. "Ha! what sight checks their speed, and turns their laughter first into silence, then into shrieks?" There's a man lying, face downward, in the little shallow pond that a child might have waded! To run for help, to drag the wretched creature from the water, was speedily done. There was no symptom of a struggle in the form or face—John Waverton had been dead for hours.

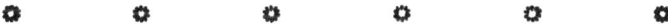

✿   ✿   ✿   ✿   ✿   ✿

"And what had become of the wife and child?" A volume would not tell the details of their sorrows and humiliations. We have only space for an outline. Both are still living. The daughter learned her business as a dressmaker, but became wholly estranged from her mother; and, two years back, emigrated to Australia, carrying with her as her only capital, a heart that never felt, and never will feel, a touch of sympathy for any creature but herself. She took no leave of her mother, and has never written to her. Extremes meet—great pampering and great misery— each produce selfishness, and the poor mortal had been tried by both.

Mrs. Waverton said something very like truth, when she exclaimed, she "could not die." "The heart may break, yet brokenly live on." She has lived in many situations, but stayed in none. Clever and quick,—not a drunkard, though a constant drinker. Her captious temper, her restlessness, the frequent anguish that overmasters and incapacitates her —for, with all her faults, she has a heart—make people glad to part with her. She has been companion, house-keeper, nurse, cook, household drudge, skilful in all, yet unendurable—her poverty has been of the bitterest. In one of the Servants' Homes of the Metropolis she has become a kind of fixture; and this very winter, an old servant of hers who recognised her, gave some cast-off clothes to shelter the once lovely Mrs. Waverton from the weather. And now, too old for service, she picks up a scanty subsistence waiting on the better class of servants in the Home. A gin drinker, but scorning the name of drunkard, the desolate widow, the heart-broken mother, has become the " servant of servants." Oh, reader! when you talk of " Ups and Downs in Life," try to trace causes as well as consequences.

OUR YOUNG MINISTER.

"For after that a man soweth,
Thereafter that he moweth,
And every man's doom to his own door cometh."
KING ALFRED'S *Proverbs.*

"You'll take a glass of wine, Sir! I'm sure, after all your fatigues yesterday—just one glass—it wont hurt you—it's very choice sherry—Mr. Mainwaring?" said Miss Penelope Masham. "Papa's as good a judge of wine as of a sermon," added her niece, Fanny Masham, laughingly passing the waiter from her aunt's hand, and approaching the chair where the young minister was timidly hesitating out a refusal of the proffered hospitality.

"Nonsense! now *do!*" was blandly reiterated by both ladies; and so, the gentleman looking from one to the other, and shuffling uneasily in his chair, and colouring violently, took the wine, still muttering apologies. "It was so early." "He never did take any." "It was only by the rarest chance." "Really, as you are so pressing," and then the sparkling mischief was in his hand, and to his lips. Just as he had finished his glass, a visitor was announced—Miss Freeman, and a look of great annoyance was visible on the faces of aunt, niece, and visitor, as the lady entered the room; indeed, there was for a moment a kind of nervous motion of Fanny's hand, as if she would throw an antimacasser, snatched from the end of the couch, over the decanter and glasses; but the action was momentarily checked, and a little defiant look mounted with the colour to her brow; while Miss Penelope infused a colder chill into her icy smile and rigid form, and Mr. Mainwaring looked very much like a thief caught in the fact.

"I fear my visit is ill-timed," said the lady in a frank, cheerful voice, evidently at a glance comprehending both the awkwardness of the company and its cause.

With the most polite insincerity, the niece and aunt said, "Oh, dear no, delighted to see you!" Mr. Mainwaring, with the flavour of the wine in his throat, coughed, bowed, and said nothing. The lady briefly introduced the object of her visit—to ask subscriptions to maintain a Temperance Missionary.

"A Temperance Missionary!" said both ladies, the one with a toss of her head that set all her curls shaking as if to prove the lightness of the ball they adorned, the elder with a little sneer curving her thin lips.

"Mr. Mainwaring, I had calculated on your recommending our friends to aid in this work," said Miss Freeman in a tone of disappointment as her eyes glanced from him to the decanter on the table. "You know how, in this suburb of London it is needed."

The young minister coughed again, cleared his throat and uttered an awkward assent.

"Oh, Mr. Mainwaring is not fond of crotchets; he takes enlightened views," said Miss Penelope; her niece assenting with the words, "Certainly he does."

"Pardon me, Miss Masham, it is surely no crotchet to say intemperance prevails greatly, and no folly to try to remedy it."

"Oh, such a sermon as we had last night!" said Fanny, her curls vibrating as she spoke—"that's the remedy, dear Miss Freeman!"

"Take up your cross and follow me," said the aunt, turning up her eyes devoutly as she repeated the text of the admired discourse.

"Yes," replied Miss Freeman, "take up your cross," and somehow her eyes, in turning from the decanter and glasses, met those of the minister. He blushed to his very temples, and the lady, pitying his evident confusion, added quickly, —"And how many of the poor, the ignorant, and the intemperate were there to hear the sermon? I saw plenty of satin and broadcloth—where were the stuff gowns and fustian coats? Ah me, they were in garrets, cellars, or worse —in gin-palaces and tea-gardens, getting, poor things! the worst of both worlds, and none to care for them."

Just at this moment, a stout gentleman, with a ponderous walk and a ponderous voice, slow and unctuous, entered the room and paused to hear the last words before he came to the table and offered his salutations, adding, "Ah, my dear Sir! our esteemed friend Miss Freeman has great zeal, but she goes too fast and too far. She'll pardon my frankness; she knows my mind." "Now," he continued, "as to there being 'none to care for them,' that's not fair, Miss Freeman. I and my family—we are but three, you know—subscribe to the Bible Society, the Tract Society, to all the local charities—and only just this very morning, I have subscribed to the Distressed Needlewomen's Society. We help the poor, and what more can be done?"

"Much, Mr. Masham! teach the poor to help themselves —prevent poverty."

"Prevent poverty! ah, that's the preposterous nonsense of the socialists. It's Divinely said, 'The poor ye have always with you.'"

"Certainly, Sir! infancy, age, sickness, and misfortune— these are sacred demands on our sympathies. Such cases there will always be—need we add to them in numbers, and take from God's inevitable poor, to give to the wicked and the profligate — nay, make laws to tempt to crime, and poverty, and destitution? But I need not take up your time, Sir, my question is soon asked; a few friends want to engage a Temperance Missionary to go among the working-classes, and by his example and precept try to prevent their spending their hard earnings in buying poverty, disease, and death."

"Oh, I could'nt—I am sorry to refuse a lady and a valued friend, but I dare not put anything of man's device before the people. For man's device is often the devil's device."

Again Miss Freeman looked at the decanter, and her eyes said pretty plainly, "That is a device of sinful man and his master." But her efforts, she saw, were fruitless, and with

a pained look round the circle, that increased in pensiveness
as she glanced at the young minister, she took leave of
them.

Of course, there was a due declaiming on "crotchety
people," "wholesale morality," "new fangled fashions,"
" old maid's projects," &c., &c., when the lady had departed;
but there was one of the company who could not join in the
conversation, and was heartily glad when it was over. Mr.
Mainwaring felt himself condemned. By his weakness, he
had strengthened the family he visited in dangerous habits,
and lost the privilege of helping a cause he knew to be good.
The sacred right of denouncing error and speaking truth he
had sold Esau-like for a momentary gratification. Nay,
worse, the fear of ridicule, the difficulty of withstanding the
smiling urgency of his fair temptress had overcome him.
He left their house execrating himself—feeling gloomy and
despondent. No company was so disagreeable at that moment as his own, as he continued his calls; and, at every
house he entered, praises of his sermons of the previous
Sabbath were mingled with invitations to take wine, all the
more pressingly urged because it was Monday and he must
be languid. He refused, honestly owning that he had already
taken a morning glass of wine; and as he returned to his
own lodgings, he reflected, that, if he had taken the half of
the wine offered him that day, he would have been in no
condition to walk home. And then there came to his recollection the painful fact that his predecessor, for years a minister of good repute, for holy life and valuable services, had
made shipwreck of name and fame—overcome by the foe
that biteth like a serpent, and stingeth like an adder. It
was a short, sad story:—Ephraim Pliant had been very popular in the pulpit and out. He was excitable, and had been
advised to smoke as a sedative. He was often languid and
low-spirited, and he was recommended the moderate—oh, of
course, the moderate use of stimulants. One of his "dear
people" was a brewer, and the minister's increased size and
glowing cheek was quite an advertisement of the merits of
his deacon's beer. Another of his "leading friends" was a
wine merchant, and as he also dutifully wished to have a
share in amending his minister's health, he sent him many

presents of choice wine, which the minister in return could recommend to retired tradesmen grown dyspeptic, and to ladies who wanted something to do, and who never read, or never heeded the stern bard's admonition:—

> "Observe what ills to nervous females flow,
> When the heart flutters, and the pulse is low,
> If once induced these cordial cups to try,
> All feel the ills, and few the danger fly;
> For while obtained, of drams they've all the force,
> And when denied, then drams are the resource."—*Crabbe.*

There were some among the congregation who now and then thought that as the minister habituated himself to the spirituous, he lost something of the spiritual, but they hardly liked to whisper this even to themselves. At last, death entered the house of Ephraim Pliant, and removed the wife, who, for seventeen years had spread the mantle of her love over her husband's failings. She left him one daughter nearly sixteen years of age; and the dying woman's last earthly thought was pleasant; for Miriam would, she believed, supply her place in the house, and take the charge of providing for her father's comforts. But the young girl could not cope with the difficulties that soon surrounded her. Long hours after Miriam had retired to rest, her father was smoking and sipping in his study, and Martha, the maid servant, who had lived years with them was now indispensable, for she understood, as she said, "Master's health, and his nerves, and mixed his night cap to a T;" and so matters rested until there were whispers that Martha was flushed and saucy, that Miss Miriam was snubbed by her—that the minister was not alone in his study late at nights; and all these whispers gathered together till they made a cry that resounded far and wide, and the degraded man and disgraced minister became, too late for honour, the husband of a low, ignorant woman, and of course had to leave, none being more disgusted and indignant than the brewer and the wine merchant. For months, Deptford Street Chapel was without a regular minister. Many supplies had come and gone, when Mr. Mainwaring, a student with more Greek and Latin than common sense, seemed likely to settle among them.

Now, it would be very hard to blame this young man for so general a defect as that hinted at. Why, of all the rare things in this world, common sense is the rarest! Learning, and talent, and virtue, are as gold and silver, standard—solid and valuable; common sense is a diamond that cuts its bright way through all obstacles, and reflects in its beaming ray the unclouded light of truth.

It was some amends for the young minister's folly of the morning that he despised himself for it. But how to meet Miss Freeman, whose character he so respected, how to face a few of his poorer members, who had struggled against both custom and appetite, and were trying to hold out a helping hand to miserable beings whose feet had slipped in the path of the inebriate. How could he write to one fair correspondent, whose words of gentle counsel had been, "Avoid all tampering with the drinking customs of society, as you would avoid ruin and death."

But then that Fanny Masham! with her rosy smiles, and her pale, golden curls, that she knew so well how to shake in the sunlight till her head glittered like a star. Ah! all is not gold that glitters, young man! and there's that quiet, unobtrusive Esther Firmly, whom you have known from boyhood, and whose words of wisdom, prompted by a loving heart and sound brain, you would do well to ponder. And so it seemed the young minister thought, for as he sat alone he took out a letter from his desk, and as he read it, the remembrance of the lovely feather-brain passed away, and he groaned in spirit over the yielding of the morning.

It might be that our young minister would not have shown the sincerity of his convictions as to true sobriety, nor have withstood the temptations which lie thick in the path of every young man, and, perhaps, thickest in that of a minister (for he is tempted to add hypocrisy to sin), but for an incident which occurred that week. Miss Freeman was one of those women—may their number increase!—who thought that works of mercy and wisdom were as good a pursuit in life as Berlin wool and crotchet, and as amusing as lap-dogs and parrots, and nearly as stimulating as fashion and scandal; and though she had a thoroughness about her which must be called by the awful epithet "strong-minded," she did not limit her efforts to do good on any special plan. She had her idea, and very firmly it was rooted in her mind, that a sober community, could the world once see such a thing, would have but little need of jails, or pauper houses, or lunatic asylums, or any of the thousand and one plans by which the gentle hand of order and benevolence picks up those the armed hand of sin has flung down. So while she patronised the temperance cause as the great cure, she aided also many good plans that dealt with effects rather than causes. And the claims of "Distressed Needlewomen" were not forgotten by her. She met in this society, as in every other, with intemperance as a cause of misery, and found that her theory of the number of innocent victims of the national vice was fully borne out by facts.

On the very evening in which she had encountered our young minister at Mr. Masham's, and had been so pained by seeing the same temptation employed that had ruined the former pastor, she received a letter that very much distressed her; it contained tidings of one she had known for a short time, for Miss Freeman had not long resided in London, and only casually had met the minister, whose fall we have recorded. Early, the morning after she received the letter, she set out from Dulwich Street, North, and traversing London, went to a court in Bedford Bury. A dirty looking woman, who answered to the name of Pliant, and who, even at that early hour, was odorous of gin, piloted the lady up three pair of stairs to a back room, and there told a dismal story of the distress of her husband, once the minister of Deptford Street Chapel, and made many complaints against her daughter-in-law, Miriam. "Where are they both?" said Miss Freeman. "Oh! her husband was gone out to see a gentleman, hoping to get some employment, and Miriam was taking home some needlework, but she had been paid for it beforehand, and the grate was fireless and the cupboard empty." There was no disbelieving the fact of great poverty, for all around was desolate.

It was a keen March day, and the east wind was piercing even to the joints and marrow, but something in the woman's manner induced Miss Freeman to doubt her testimony. "I should like to see Mr. Pliant," she said, "or his daughter; I know him, and I think I have seen her, but I do not recollect you." "No, we left soon after you came," said the woman, which was indeed the truth; and she added, "He's not able to walk far, Miss."

"Well," replied Miss Freeman, putting five shillings into her hand, "I'll call again this evening." "Please, ma'am, not to-night, to-morrow would be better," said the woman, grasping the money with a kind of clutch. "Very well, I'll think of it," said Miss Freeman, drawing her cloak around her as she descended the dilapidated stairs and faced the wind. The keen blast making her feel, if possible, more intensely for the suffering of the poor, it occurred to her that if she could get a companion she would call again in the evening and try to see either father or daughter—the woman's putting her off at that time all the more confirming her in her purpose. But who was to be her companion? She thought of the young minister, and it may be the hope of doing him good by showing him the wreck that had split on the very rock he was, to her thinking, steering for, made her decide on sending 'for him, and asking him to bear her company on her errand. She knew he was pious, diligent, amiable, but he wanted the watchfulness that keenly looks out for "breakers a-head," and the bravery to steer a new course.

Mr. Mainwaring was startled at receiving the summons of Miss Freeman, fancying that she was going to use the privilege of her sex and years, and lecture him about Monday morning; and his masculine pride was rather roused by the thought of being "schooled." Ah! Miss Freeman knew human nature too well to make a dead set at the young minister; she never alluded to the incident at Masham's, but contented herself with relating her visit to Bedford Bury, and her wish to investigate farther than the woman had told her. Most willingly he agreed to be her escort, and as soon as night had fallen, they set out on their exploring expedition. There are few districts of London that present more unmistakable evidence of the effects of the national sin than Bedford Bury and its purlieus. Courts and alleys, reeking with every abomination of rags and filth, intersect "The Bury," as the main street is called, and in the latter, gin-shops, tobacconists, and sellers of filthy prints are the most flourishing trades. Most of the other shops are mean, and the provisions coarse; the flaring tavern and palace rob the working man of the light that should illume his home, and the food that should be upon his table. The two companions made their mental comments as they passed the ragged children that scuffled on the pavement, and the filthy women that lounged at the corners, or passed in and out of the drinking houses, while the voice of ribald blasphemy or brutal riot resounded in all directions. It was with a beating heart that the young minister followed the steps of Miss Freeman, up the court and into the open door of the dingy house she entered. Without interruption they climbed the stairs, and nearly falling over a pail, flanked by a broken-nosed pitcher, that stood on the landing, they knocked at the door of the room Miss Freeman had visited in the morning, but received no answer, and on trying it they found it fastened. There was, however, the sound of breathing near, and Miss Freeman thought it was a sleeping child, but presently a thin gasping voice called down the stairs from an attic floor above, and asked "Who was there?" The friends with difficulty ascended what was more like a steep ladder than a staircase into a garret in the roof. Only in the centre could Mr. Mainwaring stand upright, and it took some moments to accustom his eyes to the light of a feeble candle that was mounted on a box by the side of what seemed a heap of rags in a corner. Something moved in the midst of the heap. Miss Freeman, with a hesitating step, drew near and looked intently: it was with difficulty she suppressed a scream, as in the wasted form and pallid face of a young girl, who was sitting on the floor wrapped round by the poor rags to keep her warm, she recognised the almost childish features of Miriam Pliant. A black silk skirt, the seams of which she was running, concealed her own tattered garb, and left only the thin hands and wrists worn to the bone, and the slender palpitating throat, exposed to view.

"Can it be possible!" said Miss Freeman. "Is it indeed Miriam?"

"Who are you?" said the young girl, her heart beating so as to impede her feeble utterance. "I do not know you —leave me," she added, "to my fate."

Miss Freeman was not surprised that she was not recognised, for her intercourse had been most casual with both the minister and his daughter, and the latter with her memory full of the faces of well known friends, had not retained such a recollection of Miss Freeman's features as to make a recognition instantaneous.   But when she heard the name, then her head dropped—she threw herself mournfully down and pulled the skirt like a pall over her, and the silence of the room was broken by her sobs.   As soon as she could command voice she said passionately, " Go away, go away."

It was then Miss Freeman assured her they wished to do her good, and gently asked why she had been written to, if her coming was considered an intrusion.

" I never wrote to you," said the young girl, at length raising her head and putting aside her work.   " I wrote at my poor father's wish months ago to Mr. Loftus and Deepdrain (the wine merchant and the brewer), and, on my own account, I did also write to Miss Penelope Masham.   Mr. Loftus never answered us, Mr. Deepdrain sent us a tract on ' The Work of the Holy Spirit,' and Miss Masham told me, I ought to have let her know in time how things were going on, and that my father and I were justly punished.   As if I knew," said she bitterly, " how things were going on myself until the storm burst."   A fit of coughing at this juncture so shook the feeble frame of the young girl that the awe-struck spectators trembled for the consequences.   The sufferer, half strangled, pointed to a medicine bottle on the window-sill.   Miss Freeman, seeing neither cup nor glass gave it to her, and the young girl put it to her lips and gulped it down.

" What is it ?" asked Mr. Mainwaring, speaking for the first.

" Gin," gasped the poor creature, adding as she regained her voice, " That serves for food and physic to outcasts like me."

" Where's your father, my poor child," said Miss Freeman.

" In St. Luke's workhouse; he's been there these ten weeks."

" And your moth— that is Mrs. Pliant."

" Dead ———— some friends in the north who pitied my father, sent him twenty pounds last Christmas, and she drank hard, fell down and cut her head, and died in Westminster Hospital of erysipelas."

"Then, who is it writes letters in her name?" "I know not, unless it's the begging letter-writer on the first-floor, who sets the woman that boils the kettle for us to find out any names we may mention. She knew all about my father's miserable wife."

"Who do you mean by *us?*" said Mr. Mainwaring.

"Why, Ellen and Kate who lodge with me."

Miss Freeman hesitated a moment and then said—"What are Ellen and Kate."

"Dressmakers—that is skirtmakers when they can get it, —but this winter—oh, this winter—don't ask me—I can tell you no more," and a cold chill ran through her frame.

To procure some food, and get a little girl from a neighbouring cobbler's room, as the most trustworthy person they could find, to make a basin of gruel for the poor girl, was all that could be done. To move her then, weak as she was, in the bleak, night air, was a risk, that until they had considered the case, they could not hazard.

"And this is all the doing of strong drink," said Miss Freeman, as she and her companion walked to the omnibus. Mr. Pliant's reputation was his life—that gone, he was ruined totally. Unfit for any other pursuit than that which he had disgraced, it did not seem wonderful that he should have drank deeper than ever to allay the pangs of remorse; and that his brain should have maddened with his fall. That the ignorant woman, at once tempter and victim, should have died in consequence of her besetting sin, was but a fulfilment of the Scripture, "He that pursueth evil, pursueth it to his own death." But Miriam, the young, the motherless, the innocent! That she also should have been drawn into the vortex, was indeed dreadful; and through the long hours of the night, Miss Freeman kept revolving plans for her rescue. The most feasible seemed to get her into the Consumptive Hospital if possible, and thus to remove her from her present den of misery and guilt.

That night, Mr. Mainwaring wrote to Esther Firmly, told of his weakness, and mentioned his resolve, that the time past should suffice for irresolution and trimming; for the future he would be as decided for the practice as he was for the doctrines of that religion which says, "To

him that knoweth to do good, and doeth it not, to him it
is sin."

The next day, and the next, found Miss Freeman at the
miserable lodging of poor Miriam.　Gradually she had
soothed the irritated feelings of the sufferer smarting under
a sense of her father's humiliation, and the "rich man's con-
tumely," not the more easy to bear, because those who showed
it called themselves the excellent of the earth.

Poor Miriam's story was, after all, but a common one—
yes, reader! if you have ever gauged the deeps of the social
degradation of a great city, you will know it was but a common one.　"Pshaw! I'll not believe it—it's an exaggeration.
A minister's daughter running seams in a garret, the companion of disreputable women!　I'll not believe it."　Very
well, good madam, yours is the reasoning of the ostrich,
who, when pursued, hides his silly head in the sand, and
because he can see nothing, thinks that all are as blind and
dark as himself.　Go to the hospital, the workhouse, or the
penitentiary, and you may hear if you will, young creatures,
one after another, declare that their father or their mother
drank, poverty came on; they were not fit for servants, not
trained for teachers, not put in any comfortable way to learn
respectably and safely the business of millinery or dressmak-
ing.　Money, connections, decent clothing, were all needed.
So, as day-workers to grinding, slaving, mantle or skirtmakers,
they begin to earn their bread.　The stimulus of gin is used
in the workroom to rouse their flagging energies—to spur
their jaded spirits.　Then comes the night walk home and
its snares, hungry, tired, conscious of being hard worked and
ill paid.　Is the horrible sequel so marvellous?　It's well
for a very great deal of first-class virtue in this world that it
never knew anything of such fiery trials.

Miriam did not live to be admitted into the hospital.

She died a week afterwards in the infirmary of —————
Parish Workhouse.　Miss Freeman was with her at the last.
She had learned the few particulars of the sad history.　The
family had lived on her father's books and household furniture for three months, then they moved from one lodging to
another, running down the entire gradations of poverty.　At
last Miriam, stung by her mother-in-law's reproaches of her

idleness, got work where she could—too poor and too friend-less to make much choice. Christmas, its gift and its riot followed, then death! madness! and the poor child was left alone among the companions poverty and chance had intro-duced to her. She had no kindred in England; an aunt, the wife of a missionary, was her only relative. Her letters to former friends had been repulsed: so hungered and angered, poor Miriam sunk to the level to which her father's intem-perance had dragged her. And surely it was in mercy that the winter's cold had chilled her young blood and laid her on the friendly bed of death. Something of the good seed sown in early days by her mother's hand sprung up, and showed itself as she neared the dark river; she did not say much, but once after a long silence she asked Miss Freeman a ques-tion uttered in an eager voice,—"Do you think He will say to me 'Thy sins be forgiven thee?'" "Yes! my poor child, if with all your heart you trust in Him," was the tear-ful reply. There was a little fluttering smile went wandering over the pale face at the words; the weary head nestled down in the pillow like a child seeking its mother's breast, and a deep sleep came on that knew no awakening. Ah! poor outcast on thy pauper bed! it shall be more tolerable for thee at the day of judgment, than for multitudes who walk in pride, and thank God because they are not like others.

From this time, a change came over "our young minister." He not only refused glasses of wine at morning calls, but he refused them at dinner, and he equally rejected beer and spirits, and his "leading friends" wondered what ailed him; but they only whispered their surprise, until he began to warn them in private, and proceeded from that to speak pub-licly against the drinking customs, and from less to more actually ventured to organize a Temperance Society among the congregation, and went forth with other zealots to seek the wandering inebriate in the streets and waysides, and "compel them to come in." This was too bad. Mr. Loftus, and Mr. Deepdrain, and Mr. Masham could stand it no longer. They could wink at the foibles of a smoking, drinking minister as long as he kept pretty straight before the world, but this "rash workmonger," this "vulgar zealot," "consorting with low people and ruining the respectability of a genteel congregation! it was unbearable. He should go or they would." But the majority chose him, and he felt he ought not to go. Then they would leave him with a heavy debt on the building to fight his way as he could. So in great dudgeon they withdrew, the gentlemen to find a minister who was "sound," that is to say, who thought and acted as they did, and the ladies to try their blandishments, and Miss Fanny in particular her curls, on a dear pastor who was gentlemanly, and bland, and sympathizing in his tastes and manners, and who had no impertinent country engagement with any Esther Firmly.

The mention of that last young lady's name renders it necessary to say that she did not take possession of the Chapel House until nearly two years after the events of our narrative. She had an old-fashioned notion that those principles are the strongest that time and trial have tested, and when she found that Mr. Mainwaring bore the desertion of his richest members, the censures of brother ministers, and the constant toil of labouring among the poor, and that instead of murmuring he was hopeful and resolute, then she thought his argument that a pastor's house was unfurnished without a wife, had some truth in it, and Miss Freeman soon after welcomed one who proved indeed a helpmate to "our young minister."

A NARROW ESCAPE.

THE best apology that I know for telling my story, is that it may do good to others. This is my motive in unfolding the experiences of a brief, yet stormy, period of my life. I shall be perfectly frank in all particulars, except names of persons and places; these, for obvious reasons, will be assumed.

Mine was an orphan childhood. My aunt, Miss Jane Garty, had brought me up conscientiously rather than tenderly, and I respected, though, I am free to own, I did not love her. I loved my nurse, Mary, dearly. She used to tell me stories of my mother, and describe her illness and death so circumstantially, that, as I grew up, her words seemed like the promptings of my own memory, and I felt as if I had witnessed the scenes she depicted. But of my father she would say nothing, except now and then, when I sorely teazed her with my questions as to how my mother bore his loss? what sort of a man he was? She would say, petulantly, "Loss! I never could see he was much loss. She was too good for him. Poor lady! But she did not think so; she was, like many gentle creatures I've known, foolish in her love."

Beyond this I could get no information. Yet, somehow, as I grew in years, my dead mother's sorrowful love was a secret source of romantic interest to my girlish thoughts. Women sacrificing themselves for the objects of their affection, pining over unrequited love, or dying martyrs to their fidelity, was my favourite ideal. Little did my aunt suspect, as day by day I sat at her work-table, and silently heard her wonted strictures on the romantic follies of youth, the delusions of love, and the sorrows of marriage, that I was inwardly repeating to myself—

"Oh ! what was love made for, if 'tis not the same
Through joy and through sorrow, through glory and shame."

My first conscious trouble was parting with my nurse, who, though advanced in life, to the indignation of my aunt, married Joe Humphreys, a widower with a large family, who had formerly been a rejected lover of her youth.

I was hastily entering a room one day, and heard my aunt saying, "After what you have seen, Mary, of the miseries of married life." Seeing me, my aunt stopped abruptly. I felt surprised at the allusion, as my father, to whom I thought she referred, had been her own brother, and I thought it wrong of her to allude to the errors of the dead.

On the day of my nurse's departure, my aunt never left us one moment together. It struck me Mary wanted to speak to me alone; if so, she had no opportunity. She removed to a distant town, and except an annual letter the good soul sent me on my birth-day, I heard nothing of her for years. I was thirteen when this dear, humble friend left our service, and from that time my life grew duller. I had no young companions. my aunt disliked society, and her cold, stiff manners effectually repelled all advances from the few gentry of our little town. The clergyman paid us a formal visit, once a quarter; the lawyer, Mr. Scriber, bowed familiarly, as my aunt was his client, and regularly lent us his newspaper, a civility she scrupulously returned by making over to him the annual produce of a large mulberry tree in her garden, which was no sacrifice, as my aunt disliked the fruit. Once the wine merchant, who was our nearest neighbour, sent my aunt, at Christmas, a hamper of what he called samples of some choice wines and *liqueurs*. It arrived while we were out walking; and I never shall forget the look of supreme contempt with which my aunt, spurning the hamper with her foot, sent it back, saying, "My compliments to Mr. M'Mingle, as I neither want to poison nor to be poisoned, I have no use for his choice doses."

From that time, Mr. M'Mingle used to look at her with a pitying smile; and I once heard him saying to an acquaintance, in a grave, Scottish accent, "Puir leddy! it's easy seen she has a bee in her bonnet."

I confess my aunt's eccentricities prevented her good qualities being justly valued by myself or others, and though she reared me free from the contamination of the drunkard's drink, she could not be said to recommend the principle of total abstinence. It was with me merely a matter of diet. I early learned the lesson that people to be useful must be loved—to be loved, must be lovable.

In my nineteenth year I obtained leave to attend a new-year's party at Mr. Scriber's. It was a great event to me. I considered it my first entrance into society, yet some things happened to mar my comfort; my aunt would not let me have a new dress, and my only silk frock, though modernised and enlarged with all the skill of our country dressmaker, was so tight and scanty that I looked, to my mortification, like a great girl grown out of my clothes.

However, youth needs but little embellishment; and my aunt, in reply to my murmur against my dress, as I took leave of her, said, with more fondness than I had ever known her to express, "With those clusters of chestnut ringlets, bright eyes, and rosy cheeks, you want no finery. Nature has been profuse enough in decorating the outside of the head, if only the inside corresponded."

It was an important night to me. There was a gentleman there, a surgeon, from the fashionable town of Stoke Cotswold. This Mr. Endean was about eight years my senior. He was on a Christmas visit to Mr. Scriber, who had what the Germans call "a daughter-full-house;" and who, on this occasion, had assembled a host of young bachelors from far and near. Mr. Endean was more an intelligent than a handsome man; but none seemed to me so gentlemanly and agreeable. With ready feminine instinct, I saw that the young ladies of the house pitied my unfashionable dress, and patronised me as if I was a child—my simple costume having indeed the effect of making me look much younger than I really was. Being timid and embarrassed, I suppose I felt grateful that Mr. Endean singled me out and paid me marked

attention.   Nor could I help being flattered by overhearing
him say in reply to some ill-natured remark of Mrs. M'Mingle
(who never had forgiven the rejection of the hamper), "I
quite differ from you.   I find it refreshing in this pretentious
world to meet with manners so simple and natural."

From that night, Mr. Endean occupied my thoughts much
more than my aunt would have approved.   Stoke Cotswold
was not more than ten miles distant, and he often rode over
on Saturday night and staid for the Sunday morning's service at our church.   There I saw him, for our pew adjoined
that of the Scribers.   I could hardly think the eloquence of our
clergyman attracted him, and a rumour went that he came
to visit one of the Misses Scriber; but which, the gossips of
our town of Clackham could not decide.

Our homeward route from church was the same, and thus
there seemed nothing out of the ordinary course that we
should converse and become intimate.   However limited a
girl's society and reading may be, yet there is no way of
shutting out thoughts of courtship and marriage.   My very
isolation and reserve made me dwell on every word and incident pertaining to Mr. Endean—nor was I slow to perceive
that there was a certain coolness which had replaced the former civilities of the Misses Scriber.   I was a favourite with
their father, or I felt assured they would have dropped me
entirely.   This demeanour of theirs, more than anything in
Mr. Endean's manner, made me aware I was no longer a
mere nonentity in our little circle.

In the midst of these matters, trivial to relate, but important to me, my aunt, whose health had long been precarious,
became suddenly extremely ill.   I must do myself the justice to say that this illness of hers completely roused me
from my vain and personal fancies and feelings.   I thought
only of the friend and relative who had encumbered herself
with my orphan childhood, and who, though not fond of
children, had, to the best of her ability, brought me up, and
given me some advantages and accomplishments she had not
herself possessed.

For some weeks, I was her constant attendant.   At length
the medical men agreed, apparently in default of any other
remedy, to recommend the waters at Stoke Cotswold.   My

aunt, who had grown restless as her malady increased, acqui-
esced. I wrote to an agent to secure us lodgings, and a few
days saw us removed to the Mall near the central spa of that
pleasant town.

The removal of residence was a great event to us both;
for I very clearly remembered my aunt travelling a long distance with me when I was a child, and taking up her abode
in Clackham—a stranger among strangers.

It was desirable that my aunt should have no stairs to
mount, and our lodgings consisted of two large front parlours looking on the Mall, and shaded by its trees. It was
the end of May, and the limes before our windows were in
all the beauty of the first tender green of their delicate
leaves. Our windows opened over the grassy terrace that
sloped down into the road. I had an adjoining chamber,
with windows overlooking the rear of the house. This room
had been intended for my aunt, but she so enjoyed the view
of the Mall and its gay groups, that she resolved, notwith-
standing some fears about noise, to have a front bed-room.

It was wonderful how she rallied for a time, though we
both knew her case was hopeless. She passed some hours
of every day in her bath chair drawn up and down the Mall,
I walking by her side, and both of us enjoying the pleasant
shade of the over-arching lindens. Mr. Endean's house was
at some distance; he was not my aunt's medical man, and
though I knew he was acquainted with our residence, I was
not displeased that, in a place where I was a stranger, he
did not way-lay my walks, or seek any clandestine inter-
views. I had received one letter from him, very plain as to
his intentions: stating, that "as soon as my aunt was sufficiently recovered to see him, with my consent, he wished to
ask permission to his addressing me as a suitor." So far,
all had been open, plain, happy, clear as a calm summer's
day, and sometimes, with girlish perversity, I wished for a
little more romance, if it was merely to establish the favourite maxim, "The course of true love never did run smooth."
Not long after I received this letter, a strange incident occurred. My aunt was being wheeled one sultry evening along
the Mall in her chair. I was leisurely walking with a book
in my hand at her side. When just in a part of the pro-

menade where the throng was thickest, my aunt stretched out
her arm and made a clutch at my scarf, uttering meanwhile
a cry so loud, sharp, and distinct, that I involuntarily clasped
her in my arms, thinking she must have been suddenly
struck in some way. Nothing but a stab or a shot, it seemed
to me, could account for such a shriek. She did not utter
another sound; but lay back in her chair, trembling from
head to foot, and ghastly pale, with one hand over her eyes,
as if to shut out some frightful sight.

"What is it? What is the matter?" was the inquiry of
the startled loungers on the Mall, as they gathered round
her chair. I could give no reply as to the cause of the cry,
and my aunt sunk into insensibility. "Take her home,"
said a deep voice among the crowd, though I was too much
alarmed to notice the speaker. I thought, however, that my
aunt, even in her swoon, started with some frightful pang;
and full of vague fears, the attendant and myself, aided by
some kind helpers, got the invalid to our lodgings.

It was a long time before consciousness was fully restored.
The medical man said it was a fit, and seemed to think it
premonitory of death. After some hours' watching by her
bed, just as the twilight of the summer's night yielded to
the soft tints of morning, my aunt, with a long sigh opened
her eyes very calmly, and speaking, for her, strongly, said,
—"What is the hour, Edith? How long have I been
worse?"

"Four o'clock," I replied, and then began to parry her
other question; but she interrupted me with the words, "I
know all about it, child—all, and while I've strength I'd
better tell you something it concerns you to know. I once
hoped to have been spared the effort, but it must be done."

"Don't fatigue yourself, aunt," I said; "wait a little;"
for I dreaded her making any exertion. "Throw up the
window, child, and put back the curtains—let me look once
more on the morning sun." I obeyed mechanically, a something in her voice forbade opposition or reply. The rosy
light of the morning fell upon the pallid face and glazing
eye of the invalid. I saw a change that awed me, in the
sharpened features, and I thought of calling assistance. She
divined my thoughts, and said, "Come here, Edith; what I

have to say is for your ear only. Come closer; stoop down; I want to whisper." Cold with dread, I obeyed, and her breath thrilled through me as she said, "Edith! I saw your father to-day."

"What," I exclaimed, "saw the dead!"

"No, child! no, alas! he is not dead—your father—your living father—your wretched father—I saw him with these eyes, changed, indeed, but your father." Like one in a dream I said, "Where, who, what is my father?"

Come closer, Edith—hush! he, your father, is a ———

I started with a wild leap from the bed, looked full at my aunt to ascertain that her mind was not wandering, and then involuntarily repeated the word—

"A convict! what can you mean?"

She cowered, and seemed to shrink and collapse in the bed, as I gasped out the hateful word. "Hush!" she said, "hush, my poor child, my dear little Edith—It's very hard; I'm not mad; I tell you truth."

"Oh why was I not told this before," I said passionately; the hot flush of shame for the first time wrapping round me like a burning mantle. "My mother," I added, "where is she?" "In her grave; her broken heart at rest, as, but for you, Edith, mine would have been long ago." There was an unwonted touch of tenderness in my aunt's manner that subdued me. I swallowed the choking sobs that swelled in my throat, dropped on my knees at her bedside, and fondling her wasted hand, leaned my head close to hers, so as to hear every whisper of her voice.

"I must be brief," she said. "My brother—my only brother, entered life with every advantage; you have heard that he was a physician. During his youth not a shadow of evil darkened his progress. Oh, those were happy days! He went to London full of energy and hope, and I, in my blind love, sometimes dared to arraign Providence that our mother was not spared to enjoy the success and popularity of her son. Our father, a superannuated naval officer still lived. We heard of my brother making influential friends in London; and being a rising man, in his occasional visits to us, we were dazzled by his success. It was our constant topic—we lived in his life. But there was one drawback.

We saw that he had left off the safe habits in which he had been reared; for our father had in his youth seen a ship, and nearly all her crew, lost through a drunken captain, and he had been a water-drinker for his whole after-life, and reared his children so.   It was a grief and alarm to him that his son had departed from the wholesome custom of his father's house.   With me, hope shut out fear; I certainly saw that his face assumed a flush higher than health, and his eyes had a restless brightness I never noticed in his youth, but the word intemperance was never whispered respecting him.   He married an orphan with large property, and set up his house in what is called good style.   News of his parties and gaieties reached our retreat, and we feared the gifts of fortune would impede his professional progress—and our fears were too true.   His medical practice declined as his habits and associates became convivial.   He was gradually but surely swept into the vortex of dissipation.   At the time of your birth, Edith, I was on a visit to his home, and my eyes were opened to the fact, that the most dangerous and odious of all vices, was his besetment.   He became acquainted with some reckless speculators on the Stock Exchange, and in the wild hope of making up his loss of professional gains by speculations, he risked your mother's fortune in schemes, not one of which proved successful.   He became a desperate man. His heated brain prevented his taking a rational view of his circumstances, while his very tenderness for his wife and child goaded him on to desperate and guilty ventures.   I returned to my father full of anxiety.   I dreaded poverty, ruin, even death; but shame and disgrace I did not think of. Oh Edith, in a year from that time he was a disgraced man! He had mixed up in some bubble insurance company.   Deliberate fraud was proved against him, and before we could comprehend the charge, he—our hope and pride was tried— a convicted felon!

"To us, as a family, reputation was as the very breath of our nostrils.   Never before had our name been sullied.   My father drooped at once.   He died before the ship that took his only son to a penal settlement sailed from our shores. His latest entreaty to me was, never to tamper with the drink that had drowned the voice of conscience in my brother, and shattered our home to ruins. I promised him, and I have kept my word. Edith!" she said, sharply rising with sudden strength on her elbow, and looking me with searching glance in the face, "will you, in the strength of prayer, make the same promise for yourself; aye, and if you marry, promise never to unite your life to one who tampers with what Robert Hall was right in calling, 'liquid death and distilled damnation.'" Awed by her vehemence, and convinced of the reasonableness of her request, "Willingly," I said. She clasped my hand in hers, and looking up, exclaimed, "Lord, keep this lamb of thy fold from wandering." Her voice sunk to a whisper, and I could not follow the words of her prayer. Suddenly a passing shadow dimmed the light of the open window. I was turning my head, and rising from my knees when I felt that a strong tremor shook the sufferer. I laid my hand on her head, but she shook it off, exclaiming as she looked towards the window, "There he is, Edith! there."

I followed her eager gaze, and rushing to the window looked out; two men, each walking quickly, were turning the corner close to our house; a call, a sort of indistinct cry was on my lips. I knew not what to say, when a gurgling sob brought me back to the bed. "I'm sure it is he. Never since a year after your mother's death have I heard from him. Oh, child! I cannot speak—ask Mary Humphreys— she knows."

I hastened to pour out a restorative medicine, and rang the bell for help, as I gave the cup to the sufferer. She tried to drink it—drew a long breath—fixed her eyes on the window, and fell into a convulsion, that, before our servant entered the room, ended in the stillness of death. I was chafing her hands, and bathing her temples, thinking she had merely fainted, when the hastily summoned medical man, after looking a moment at her, led me from the room, and said those simple words that convey so much—"It is all over."

What with grief, astonishment, and dread, my mind for some days was so perplexed that I could not think clearly. I wrote to nurse Humphreys to ask her to come to me.

I was meanwhile haunted as it seemed to me with an invisible and dreaded presence. This father, of whom I knew so much and so little—was near—a disgraced, it might be a dangerous man. I was under age—he might claim me. My aunt had heard nothing of him for years—had thought him dead—hence the shock of seeing him. How I now regretted asking her no questions. It seemed to me she had told me enough to make me miserable, no more. Then I reproached myself with permitting an effort that had been too much for the failing powers of nature.

Sometimes I doubted whether she had indeed seen her brother, whether imagination had not vividly brought his face before her mind in its dying state; for the physician told me he had expected her death would be sudden.

It would be false to say Mr. Endean held no part in the tumults of my thoughts and feelings. A first love and a first grief, were throbbing in my heart, each deepening the anguish of the other. I had all the horror of crime that a young mind trained to love virtue and truth would feel, and I knew that a barrier utterly impassable had arisen between me and the joys I had once pictured. My fair prospect was suddenly obscured by a black cloud, ready to burst into a storm that would hurl me to ruin. "Shame," "Disgrace," "A convict's daughter!" were words that pursued me like fiends.

My aunt's will bequeathed me her small property, without making any mention of any other relative. I was left for my two years of minority to the guardianship of Mr. Scriber. I shrunk from the thought of companionship with his daughters. Their gaiety—their little girlish airs of condescension—the consciousness of a terrible secret, all tortured me. To guard my secret was my determination. It had been my aunt's plan; it should be mine. Nurse Humphreys came to me, and I told her I knew something of my father's history. She supplied some missing links as to his trial, and condemnation to fourteen years' transportation—my mother's illness and death—my aunt's coming to take charge of me, and our subsequent removal to Clackham. Two letters she said were all that were ever received from my father, and in searching among my aunt's papers I found these. That of the latest date said, my father had obtained a ticket of leave to work for himself in the colony, and that he was superintending a chemist s store, and should never return to England; if he prospered, he would write annually. This was the last, and my aunt naturally concluded he was dead. The tone of these letters was gloomy, even to despair. He hoped his child might never know her father's history, and probably, but for the sudden fright, I never should—though Mary Humphreys confessed she had often strong temptations to tell me.

The evening after the funeral I was sitting alone, devising how to shape a request to my guardian to be allowed to board at a school, or to go for a time to live with my nurse, who occupied a good house in a pretty rural town—anywhere to be far from the scenes of my aunt's death, and among strangers, when my reverie was interrupted by the entrance of Mr. Endean. He had often sent to inquire for me, but I had not seen him. I meant, if possible, to see him no more.

He came towards me with a look of tender interest beaming in his face, saying, "Do not think this an intrusion. No one,"—he paused and repeated the words—"No one has felt, or can feel for your trouble as I do. I have a right to share it." He was proceeding with all the moving incoherency of passion, but I affected a coldness I did not feel, and, withdrawing my hand which he had grasped and still retained, said at once—it was too painful a subject to dally with—"The past is over and gone, and can never now be renewed; Mr. Endean, for the future we must be strangers."

He recoiled as from a blow, looked at me a moment, apprehending he had not heard aright. I repeated my words in a concentrated voice, that I felt was thick with suppressed sobs.

"Why—why," he cried, "this sudden change?"

"Ask me no questions—I cannot tell you; the last few days have indeed changed me, and all about me."

"They have taken away a relative, a protector, and left you, as I hear, lonely; is not that a reason why I may urge the claims of a devoted love, why I may be permitted to offer you another protector—a husband?"

"It cannot be. I shall never marry." He looked bewildered, paced up and down the room, while I still gasped out repeatedly the word "Never."

"You are agitated," he said at length. "I have come too abruptly upon you. You need rest; I will leave you now. Oh surely, Edith, I may hope in time for a different decision."

My nurse hearing my sobs, for they could no longer be repressed, came in at that moment, and he left. My resolution was taken; I wrote instantly to my guardian, asked to be permitted to accompany Mrs. Humphreys to her home for a time; and knowing a day must elapse before I could have a reply, desired that no one might be admitted to see me.

I employed the intervening time in writing to Mr. Endean. Oh what a work it was to struggle with the yearnings of my heart! Every fibre pleaded his cause; nay I felt it was equally my cause. "Shall I bring a dower of shame to an honourable man?" said duty. "He need never know," said inclination. "Dare I marry with such a secret untold? Shall I tell him?" Then the terror of my disgraced father hovering about the very region, knowing me, I ignorant of him. A father, perhaps not a penitent, but still active in crime. I clasped my hands over my eyes as if to shut out the thought, and panted to go away with my nurse where no eye that had once known me, should see me more—anywhere out of the vicinity of this mysterious, impending horror.

Another strong determination came. I had heard from nurse details of the wretched vice that had been the desolator of the home of my infancy, and, on my knees, I renewed the promise I had made to my dying aunt. Suddenly I recollected that Mr. Endean had once spoken sarcastically of my water-drinking; and that, without my attaching any importance to the subject, I had heard of his being convivial in his habits. "The soul of every company," I had heard him called. This was exactly the phrase that my nurse employed when she spoke of my father's habits and character. How I shrunk from the thought of the tendencies of a habit that I had now learned to consider was pleasure in the beginning, and ruin in the end.

After many attempts, I completed a letter to Mr. Endean, reiterating my refusal; and the next day bringing me my guardian's permission, I hastened my preparations, and set off with my nurse, seeking, in change, security and peace of mind—the latter, my own heart, throbbing with a weight of woe, put far from me.

For some weeks, my retirement was completely unknown, except by an occasional letter from the eldest Miss Scriber, who took occasion to tell me "Mr. Endean was strangely altered, and that some of his best friends considered he was a different man after dinner, and that such a report she thought would injure him as a medical man. She added, that he was looking ill and unhappy!"

In my low state of health and spirits, those tidings greatly distressed me. The terrible customs of society that allure only to betray, appeared to my mind in all their foul, specious, and deep enormity. A gigantic sham, made up of deceitful smiles and bland professions, seemed to me to fill the world with guilt and woe. With my eyes fully opened, I saw now in every newspaper a chronicle of the seductive vice of intemperance. I noted how it added to the poverty of the poor, the misery of the helpless, and the crime of the criminal—how it snatched the bread from famine, branded the brow of youth, paralyzed the arm of manhood. It was not enough for me that I was safe. I wanted to help, to warn, to rescue those who were fast becoming victims.

I was, for all my simple wants, amply supplied with money by my guardian. I employed my surplus means in aiding the temperance society of the district. I assisted to establish a Band of Hope, and found some comfort to my own sorrows in helping to lighten the miseries of others.

Thus more than a year passed away. Of my unknown father, I heard nothing; and I began to doubt altogether my aunt's having really seen him, when one day my retirement was broken by the sudden arrival of Mr. Endean. He looked pale and agitated; but something in his manner stayed my words, when I would have remonstrated with him on this intrusion. "Edith," he said, earnestly, "you must hear me; I come to make a confession. You see before you one who has narrowly escaped utter ruin. I need not tell you I was both grieved and mortified at your refusal. In my folly, I sought comfort or oblivion in wine; my previous habits helped this delusion. Of course, I never meant to be a drunkard; that low and loathsome thing! Of course, mine was to be merely a gentlemanly phase of wine-bibbing. Oh! Edith, with the lives of many confided to me, I dared to tamper with my bodily and mental strength. A friend, once indeed merely a humble retainer, now a friend, and the best I have ever known, warned me—risked my anger by his persevering warning—watched with sleepless fidelity my every action. In my perversity and sin, I resented this, I would have sent this friend from me; but he bore with untiring patience my petulence and insolence; he was bent on saving me, and he has. Last week, Edith, I wrote a prescription; it was for a whole family, ill of a slight epidemic attack. I sent it to my wholesale chemist, who supplied to my messenger what I had by mistake written for—a peculiar form of deadly poison, only served to medical men.

"My friend detected the error, supplied the medicine I meant to order, and retained the deadly potion until, in the morning, my reason was restored, and then he confronted me with a charge which seemed to cut the ground from under my feet. Every emotion of my soul condemned me; I dared not think of the precipice on which I stood, except to wonder, awe-struck, at the providence that snatched me from ruin. My faithful friend reproved me sternly, and concluded by telling me his history. Oh, Edith! this benefactor, whose watchfulness has saved me from bearing a murderer's guilt and doom, this benefactor is your father."

I was speechless with wonder and thankfulness. "He has saved me," he added; "I know all; I understand now the motive for conduct I once thought inexplicable; by the name of Mr. Thomas, my assistant, my friend, is known and honoured; a free man, with a spirit purified by more than the tears of penitence. He told me he had seen the name of his sister among the arrivals in our town, that he had yielded to his desire to see her, and watched you both in your walks and rides, unobserved, as he thought—for, knowing his sister's stern sense of honour, he never meant to make himself known. 'What was I,' he said, 'that the dear joy of a father or brother should be ever known by me; in the grave of my heart-broken wife, I buried the claims to all family ties, all joys of home or kindred.'

"I had also my explanations to make, my promises to give. I told him, Edith, of my love. I promised, I pledged myself to forsake at once and for ever the drink that had well-nigh destroyed me, in name and fame, body and soul. Edith, God giving me strength, I will keep that promise!" He bowed his head reverently, and we stood mute and awed with the consciousness that the words just spoken were recorded in Heaven.

I need not enter into details as to my own feelings. The cloud that had enveloped me like a pall fell off from me instantly. I was no longer alone in the world—struggling with a wounded spirit, and weighed down with the burden of life. God had heard my prayers, and opened a way by which duty and inclination would be reconciled.

My heart yearned to my father. I felt he had given me more than life, in giving me back, a rescued man, the lover of my youth. It was, too, a most blissful emotion to hear my father's name coupled with words of commendation and gratitude, to one who had so long thought herself an orphan, and more recently had learned the sad lesson, how much less painful it is to mourn a dead, than to fear a living father; it was a joy approaching to ecstacy.

I was, however, obliged to restrain my eagerness to see my long lost parent. He shrunk from the interview, and persisted in his plan of continuing unacknowledged with such pertinacity, that we feared he would go forth a wanderer among strangers, if we opposed him. So he had his way, lived at the business house, dispensing medicines as usual, and attending to the most laborious part of the practice among the poor. His skill was given chiefly to those whose health was their livelihood.

On my marriage, a house out of town was taken as a private residence. Here, for once and for all, I received the tender consecration of a father's blessing. From that time he would be simply Mr. Thomas. "I deserve no kindred; I have forfeited all rights," he said, "except the right of labour and the privilege of prayer."

And so we left it; respecting the deep penitence that, like a halo, surrounded him. Many blessings came upon our union. My husband's resolution from that fatal time was

I

firm as a rock.   His character gained in mental and spiritual power.   Our children, as they gathered round our table, learned to love not merely ourselves, *but* " dear Mr. Thomas." I see them now from my window, climbing the old man's knee, as he sits on a bench in the garden.   The setting sun has robed the group in a soft crimson glow, and touched with a brighter beam the silvered head that bends down to the youngest child.   He is dismissing them with kisses and blessings for the night.   As I gaze, the words rise to my lips—

> " All his prospects brightening to the last,
> His heaven commences ere this life be past."

MACKAY AND KIRKWOOD, PRINTERS, GLASGOW.

PERIODICALS.

Price 5s. each, Post Free, the Volumes for 1853, 1854, 1855, 1856, 1857, 1858, *and* 1859 *of*

THE SCOTTISH REVIEW;

A QUARTERLY JOURNAL OF SOCIAL PROGRESS AND GENERAL LITERATURE.

The "SCOTTISH REVIEW" is also published in Quarterly Numbers, price Four Shillings per annum, Post Free, when prepaid, and ordered from the Publishing Office in Glasgow.

WEEKLY JOURNAL

OF THE

SCOTTISH TEMPERANCE LEAGUE.

PRICE ONE PENNY.

To facilitate the transmission of the *Journal,* packets (of not fewer than four copies) will be sent *post free* to any part of the United Kingdom. By remittances being made *in advance,* parcels will be sent as under:—

4 Copies for 4d.	- - - - -	Per Quarter,	4s. 4d.
8 ,, 8d.	- - - - -	,,	8s. 8d.
12 ,, 1s. 0d.	- - - - -	,,	13s. 0d.
16 ,, 1s. 4d.	- - - - -	,,	17s. 4d.

Single stamped copies sent to any part of the kingdom for 2s. 2d. per quarter, or 4s. 4d. per half-year; these copies will be impressed with the Government stamp, so that they will be suitable for re-transmission.

The *Weekly Journal* is printed during Thursday night and Friday morning, and posted in time to reach all parts of the kingdom on Saturday.

Booksellers and News-Agents can be supplied with the *Journal* by Mr. LOVE, St. Enoch Square, Glasgow; Mr. MATHER, the Box, Edinburgh.

SCOTTISH TEMPERANCE LEAGUE, 108 HOPE STREET, GLASGOW.

www.ingramcontent.com/pod-product-compliance
Lightning Source LLC
LaVergne TN
LVHW081353060426
835510LV00013B/1804

For more information:

Gale Digital Collections: http://gdc.gale.com/

The British Library: http://www.bl.uk/